SCOTT FORESMAN · ADDISON WESLEY

Mathematics

Grade 4

Reteaching Masters/Workbook

PEARSON

Scott
Foresman

Editorial Offices: Glenview, Illinois • Parsippany, New Jersey • New York, New York

Sales Offices: Parsippany, New Jersey • Duluth, Georgia • Glenview, Illinois
Coppell, Texas • Ontario, California • Mesa, Arizona

Overview

Reteaching Masters/Workbook provides additional teaching options for teachers to use with students who have not yet mastered key skills and concepts covered in the student edition. A pictorial model is provided when appropriate, followed by worked-out examples and a few partially worked-out exercises. These exercises match or are similar to the simpler exercises in the student edition.

ISBN 0-328-04968-9

Name_____

Numbers in the Thousands

Here are some different ways to represent 2,352.

Place-value blocks:

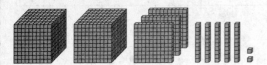

Expanded form:

2,000 + 300 + 50 + 2

2 thousands + 3 hundreds +
5 tens + 2 ones

$(2 \times 1{,}000) + (3 \times 100) +$
$(5 \times 10) + (2 \times 1)$

Standard form: 2,352   **Word form:** two thousand, three hundred fifty-two

Each digit in 2,352 has a different *place* and *value*. The digit 3 is in the hundreds place and has a value of 300.

Write each number in standard form.

1.

_____

2. 7 ten thousands + 5 thousands + 8 hundreds
+ 1 ten + 0 ones   _____

Write the word form and tell the value of the underlined digit for each number.

3. 4,6̲32   _____

_____

4. 7̲,129   _____

_____

5. 13,57̲2   _____

_____

6. Number Sense Write a six-digit number with a 5 in
the ten thousands place and a 2 in the ones place.   _____

Understanding Greater Numbers

Here are different ways to represent 555,612,300.

Place-value chart:

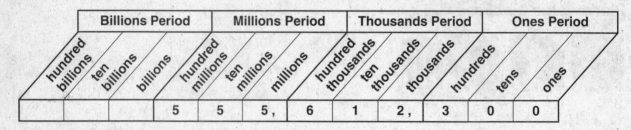

Billions Period			Millions Period			Thousands Period			Ones Period		
hundred billions	ten billions	billions	hundred millions	ten millions	millions	hundred thousands	ten thousands	thousands	hundreds	tens	ones
			5	5	5,	6	1	2,	3	0	0

Expanded form: 555,612,300 = 500,000,000 + 50,000,000 + 5,000,000 + 600,000 + 10,000 + 2,000 + 300

Word form: 555,612,300 = five hundred fifty-five million, six hundred twelve thousand, three hundred

The 6 is in the hundred thousands place. Its value is 600,000.

1. Write nine hundred seventy-six million,
   four hundred thirty-three thousand,
   one hundred eleven in standard form. _____

2. Write 80,000,000 + 700,000 + 30,000 +
   200 + 90 + 7 in standard form. _____

3. Write the word form and tell the value of the underlined
   digit in 33<u>7</u>,123,421.

   _____

   _____

   _____

4. **Number Sense** In the number 213,954,670,
   which digit has the second greatest value?
   What is its value? _____

Name_____

Place-Value Patterns

Here are two different ways to show 1,400.

One Way: **Another Way:**

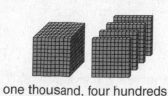

one thousand, four hundreds

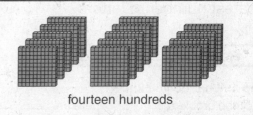

fourteen hundreds

Here are two different ways to write 660.

660 six hundred sixty   or   **660** sixty-six tens

Here are two different ways to write 40,000.

40,000 forty thousand   or   **40,0**00 four hundred hundreds

---

Name each number in two different ways.

1. 700   _____

2. 1,700   _____

_____

3. Number Sense How many tens are in 6,430?   _____

The cafeteria has 900 food trays. How many stacks of trays would there be if the trays were stacked in

4. hundreds? _____   **5.** tens? _____

6. Christopher has a collection of 1,742 pennies. If he gets 300 more, how many total pennies will he have?   _____

Look for a pattern. Find the next three numbers.

7. 2,950 3,050 3,150 _____ _____ _____

8. 1,211 1,221 1,231 _____ _____ _____

Name_____

Read and Understand

Seven Days There are seven days in a week. Each day has a certain number of letters. Which day of the week has the greatest number of letters?

Read and Understand

Step 1: What do you know?

- Tell the problem in your own words.

  There are seven days in a week, each with a certain number of letters.

- Identify key facts and details.

  The days of the week are: Sunday, Monday, Tuesday, Wednesday, Thursday, Friday, and Saturday.

Step 2: What are you trying to find?

- Tell what the question is asking.

  We want to know which day of the week has the greatest number of letters.

- Show the main idea.

Sunday	6	Thursday	8
Monday	6	Friday	6
Tuesday	7	Saturday	8
Wednesday	9		

Answer: Wednesday has the greatest number of letters.

Team Members Steve, Caroline, Heather, Brittany, Brian, Nick, Robert, Jennifer, and Susan are the players on a softball team. Are there more boys or girls on the team?

1. Identify key facts and details.

_____

_____

_____

2. Tell what the question is asking.

_____

3. Solve the problem. Write your answer in a complete sentence.

_____

Comparing and Ordering Numbers

You can use place value to compare two numbers. First line up the places of the numbers. Begin at the left, find the first place where the digits are different, and compare:

33,**4**14 5 hundreds > 4 hundreds,
⇓⇓ ⇓⇓
33,**5**15 so 33,414 < 33,515.

To order numbers from greatest to least, write the numbers, lining up places. Begin at the left and find the greatest digit. If necessary, continue comparing the other digits:

42,078	Continue comparing.	Write from greatest to least.
37,544	37,554	42,078
24,532	39,222	39,222
39,222	39,222 > 37,544	37,544
		24,532

Compare. Write > or < for each ◯.

1. 3,211 ◯ 4,221   **2.** 35,746 ◯ 35,645   **3.** 355,462 ◯ 535,845

4. Order the numbers from greatest to least.

62,500   62,721   63,001   61,435

_____ ; _____ ; _____ ; _____

5. Number Sense Write 3 numbers that are greater than 12,000 but less than 13,000.

_____

_____

Rounding Numbers

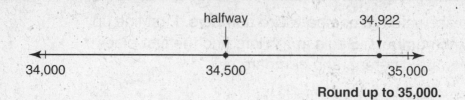

Round up to 35,000.

You can round using a number line or place value. On a number line, tell if 34,922 is closer to 34,000 or 35,000.

Using place value, find the rounding place and look at the digit to the right of it. If that digit is 5 or more, round up. If it is less than 5, round down.

For example, to round 34,922 to the nearest thousand, look at the number to the right of the thousands place. It is a 9. So, 34,922 rounds up to 35,000.

Round each number to the nearest thousand and ten thousand.

1. 13,212 _____

2. 35,645 _____

3. 55,462 _____

4. 25,845 _____

5. 367,142 _____

6. **Number Sense** Write three numbers that round to 1,000 when rounded to the nearest thousand.

_____

7. Round the population of Illinois to the nearest hundred thousand.

_____

Welcome to

ILLINOIS

Population 12,419,000

Name_____

The Size of Numbers

Small groups of numbers make up larger numbers.
You know that there are 10 dimes in $1.00.

 =

How many dimes are there in $3.00? You can skip
count to find out. 10, 20, 30.

How many dimes are in $10.00? _____100_____

Each dollar is equal to 100 pennies. How many pennies are in $10.00? ___1,000___

A box of chalk contains 10 pieces. How many pieces of chalk are in

1. 4 boxes? _____

2. 12 boxes? _____

3. 40 boxes? _____

4. Number Sense How many boxes of chalk would
you buy if you needed 500 pieces of chalk? _____

A jar holds 10,000 dimes.

5. How many $1 bills is this amount equal to?

_____

6. How many $100 bills is this amount equal to?

_____

7. How many $1,000 bills is this amount equal to?

_____

Name_____

Plan and Solve

Plenty of Words Each line of print in a children's book contains about 10 words. Each paragraph contains about 10 lines. Each page contains about 3 paragraphs. About how many words are on 10 pages of a book?

Here are the steps to follow when you plan and solve a problem.

Step 1: Choose a Strategy
- **Show what you know:** Draw a picture, make an organized list, make a table or a graph, act it out or use objects.

- **Look for a Pattern**

- **Try, Check, and Revise**

- **Write a Number Sentence**

- **Use Logical Reasoning**

- **Solve a Simpler Problem**

- **Work Backward**

Step 2: Stuck?
Don't give up. Try these.
- Reread the problem.

- Tell the problem in your own words.

- Tell what you know.

- Identify key facts and details.

- Try a different strategy.

- Retrace your steps.

Step 3: Answer the question in the problem.
What strategy can be used to solve the Plenty of Words problem?

A table can organize the information and make the problem easier.

Number of Words

1 line	10
1 paragraph	100
1 page	300
10 pages	3,000

The answer to the problem: Ten pages are equal to about 3,000 words.

Newspapers Sam usually delivers 22 newspapers each day. One day, 5 of his customers put a hold on the paper because they were going on vacation that week. Sam's boss told him that 2 new customers wanted delivery that week. How many papers did Sam deliver on the first day of that week?

1. What strategy might work to solve this problem?

_____

_____

2. Give the answer to the problem in a complete sentence.

_____

_____

Name_____

Using Money
to Understand Decimals

We can use money to understand decimals. For example, a dime is one-tenth of a dollar, or 0.1. It takes 10 dimes to equal a dollar. A penny is one one-hundredth of a dollar, or 0.01, so it takes 100 pennies to equal one dollar.

$0.01	$0.05	$0.10	$0.25	$0.50
0.01	0.05	0.1	0.25	0.5

The decimal point is read by saying "and." So, $1.99 is read as "one dollar *and* ninety-nine cents."

1. $3.52 = _____ dollars + _____ dimes + _____ pennies

2. $1.87 = _____ dollars + _____ dimes + _____ pennies

3. **Number Sense** Write nine and thirty-six hundredths with a decimal point.   _____

How could you use only dollars, dimes, and pennies to buy

4. the baseball?

_____

_____

5. the baseball bat?

_____

_____

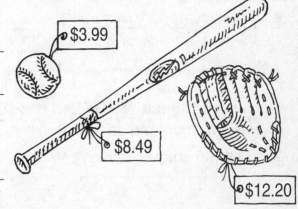

$3.99

$8.49

$12.20

Counting Money

To make an amount of money with the fewest number of bills and coins, start with the largest bill that is less than the amount you are making. For example, to make $42.26, start with the largest bill that is less than $42.26. Then keep using the largest bills or coins possible. So, we need two $20 bills, two $1 bills, 1 quarter, and 1 penny to make $42.26.

Count the money. Write each amount with a dollar sign and decimal point.

1. 3 dollars, 4 dimes, 6 pennies _____

2. 3 five-dollar bills, 8 dimes, 2 pennies _____

Tell how to make each money amount with the fewest bills and coins.

3. $5.22 _____

_____

4. $16.51 _____

_____

5. Number Sense Mr. Belford has $0.59 in a tray on his desk. He has two more dimes than quarters. What coins does he have?

_____

Making Change

An easy way to make change is to count up from the cost. For example, Chuck is making change at the convenience store. Tara buys a drink for $1.49 and pays with a $5 bill. How much change should Chuck give Tara? The chart shows how Chuck makes change.

What Chuck Does	What Chuck Says
He starts with cost of the drink.	That's $1.49
He gives one penny.	$1.50
He gives two quarters.	$1.75, $2.00
He gives three $1 bills.	$5.00
Total change given	$3.51

Chuck gives Tara $3.51 in change.

Tell how much change you would give from a $5 bill for each purchase. Give the amount with a dollar sign and a decimal point and list the bills and coins you could use.

1. $1.50 _____

_____

2. $2.73 _____

_____

3. **Reasoning** Suppose you buy an item that costs $5.03. Why might you give the salesperson $10.03?

_____

_____

_____

More About Decimals

A grid can be used to show tenths and hundredths. To show 0.3 you would shade 3 out of the 10 parts.

0.3
3 out of 10 parts are shaded.

To show 0.30 you would shade 30 out of the 100 parts.

0.30
30 out of 100 parts are shaded.

One part of the hundredths grid can be compared to a penny, since one part of the grid is equal to 0.01 and a penny is equal to one hundredth of a dollar.

Tenths and hundredths are related. In the above examples, 3 tenths or 30 hundredths of the grids are shaded, or 0.3 and 0.30. These numbers are equal: 0.3 = 0.30.

Write the word form and decimal for each shaded part.

1.

_____

2.

_____

Shade each grid to show the decimal.

3. 0.57

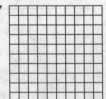

4. 0.4

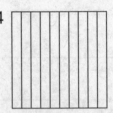

5. Number Sense Which is greater, 0.04 or 0.4? Explain.

_____

_____

_____

Name_____

Look Back and Check

Total Pins Shalyn bowled five frames, each time knocking down one pin more than the last frame. Shalyn knocked over three pins in the first frame. How many pins did she knock down after bowling all five frames?

Yoshi's Work

Frame	1	2	3	4	5
Pins Down	3	4	5	6	7
Total Pins	3	7	12	18	25

By the end of the fifth frame, Shalyn knocked down 25 pins.

You are not finished with a problem until you look back and check your answer. Here are the steps to follow.

Step 1: Check your answer.
Did Yoshi answer the right question?
Yes, she found the total number of pins Shalyn knocked down by the end of the fifth frame.

Step 2: Check your work.
Yoshi could use the pattern in her table to add numbers in the "total pins" column.

Did Yoshi use the correct operation?
Yoshi used addition to find the total pins knocked down.

Survey The results of a survey taken at Hillcrest School show that 140 students prefer bicycling as their favorite kind of exercise. There were 60 people who said swimming was their favorite. How many more students prefer bicycling to swimming?

Look back and check Yolanda's work on this problem.

Yolanda's Work

$$\begin{array}{r} 14 \\ 1\not{4}0 \\ -\ 60 \\ \hline 80 \end{array}$$

There are 80 more students who prefer bicycling.

1. Did Yolanda answer the right question? Explain.

_____

_____

_____

2. Is her work correct?

_____

Name_____

Go to the Door

Door County in Wisconsin has many small towns and miles of shoreline along Lake Michigan.

The chart shows the populations of four towns in Door County.

Town	Population
Forestville	1,680
Casco	2,066
New Franken	2,640
Fish Creek	1,200

Order the populations from least to greatest.

So, the order of the populations from least to greatest is

1,200   1,680   2,066   2,640

---

1. Algoma has a population of 5,387. Sturgeon Bay has a population of 16,149. Use these two populations and the ones in the table above to make a new list of populations from *greatest* to *least*.

   _____

2. Write the population of Forestville in expanded form.

   _____

Washington Island is near the tip of the Door County peninsula. To get there with a car or a bicycle, people have to take a ferry. Tickets for a one-way ride on the ferry cost $4.00 for adults and $2.00 for children (ages 6 to 11).

3. Jacqui bought an adult ticket and a tourist map. The total for the ticket and the map was $5.45. Jacqui paid with a $10.00 bill. How much change did she receive?   _____

Mental Math: Adding

To add using mental math, you can break apart numbers or use compensation. The Commutative Property of Addition and the Associative Property of Addition explain why this works.

$13 + 6 = 6 + 13$ Commutative Property of Addition	$(7 + 8) + 5 = 7 + (8 + 5)$ Associative Property of Addition

With **breaking apart** you can add numbers in any order.

$235 + 158$	Break apart 158. $158 = 5 + 153$
$235 + 5 = 240$	Add one part to make a ten.
$240 + 153 = 393$	Add the other part.

With **compensation** you can add or subtract to make tens.

$235 + 158$	Add 2 to make a ten. $158 + 2 = 160$
$235 + 160 = 395$	
$395 - 2 = 393$	Subtract 2 from the answer because 2 was added earlier.

Add. Use mental math.

1. $67 + 31 =$ _____

2. $29 + 43 =$ _____

3. Reasoning How can you write $72 + (8 + 19)$
to make it easier to add? _____

Marble Collection	
red	425
blue	375
green	129
yellow	99

Use mental math to find the number of

4. red and blue marbles. _____

5. red and green marbles. _____

Mental Math: Subtracting

To subtract using mental math, you can break numbers apart,
use compensation, or use counting on.

Using breaking apart

88 − 15	Break apart 15.
	10 + 5 = 15
88 − 5 = 83	Subtract one part.
83 − 10 = 73	Subtract the other part.

Using compensation

162 − 48	Add 2 to make 50.
162 − 50 = 112	2 + 48 = 50
112 + 2 = 114	Since you subtracted 2 too
	many, add 2 to the answer.

Using counting on

400 − 185	Add 5 to make 190.
	185 + 5 = 190
190 + 10 = 200	Make the next 100.
200 + 200 = 400	Add 200 to make 400.
5 + 10 + 200 = 215	Find the total of what you added.

Subtract. Use mental math.

1. 86 − 14 = _____

2. 66 − 58 = _____

3. 141 − 46 = _____

4. 206 − 78 = _____

5. Writing in Math Subtract 164 − 94, then
describe the mental math method you used.

_____

_____

_____

_____

Estimating Sums and Differences

Rounding and front-end estimation can be used to estimate sums and differences.

To estimate 1,436 + 422:

Rounding

    1,436 rounds to 1,400
    422   rounds to 400
    1,400 + 400 = 1,800

Front-end estimation

    1,400 becomes 1,000
    422   becomes 400
    1,000 + 400 = 1,400

To estimate 3,635 − 1,498:

Rounding

    3,635 rounds to 3,600
    1,498 rounds to 1,500
    3,600 − 1,500 = 2,100

Front-end estimation

    3,635 becomes 3,000
    1,498 becomes 1,000
    3,000 − 1,000 = 2,000

Estimate each sum or difference.

1. 265 + 426		**2.** 348 + 122		**3.** 562 − 223		**4.** 824 − 590	
5. 2,189 + 388		**6.** 1,329 + 5,345		**7.** 877 − 475		**8.** 9,245 − 4,033	

9. 788 + 212 = _____

10. 9,769 − 4,879 = _____

11. 65,328 − 14,231 = _____

12. 32,910 + 4,085 = _____

13. Number Sense Is 976 − 522 more or less than 400?
Explain how you can tell without actually subtracting.

_____

Overestimates and Underestimates

When you estimate, you come close to the exact answer.
If your estimate is greater than the exact answer, it is called
an overestimate. If your estimate is less than the exact answer,
it is called an underestimate.

An Overestimate	**An Underestimate**

<table>
<tr><td>3,770</td><td>rounds to</td><td>4,000</td><td>742</td><td>rounds to</td><td>700</td></tr>
<tr><td>+ 5,829</td><td>rounds to</td><td>6,000</td><td>+ 312</td><td>rounds to</td><td>300</td></tr>
<tr><td></td><td></td><td>10,000</td><td></td><td></td><td>1,000</td></tr>
</table>

Both numbers were rounded up, so 10,000 is an overestimate. The exact sum is less than 10,000.

Both numbers were rounded down, so 1,000 is an underestimate. The exact sum is greater than 1,000.

Estimate each sum or difference. Then, if
possible, tell whether your estimate is an
overestimate or an underestimate.

1. 805 − 322 _____

2. 95 + 265 _____

3. 626 + 315 _____

4. 7,774 + 2,822 _____

5. 4,555 − 2,981 _____

6. 121 + 135 _____

7. 864 − 552 _____

8. 8,103 + 6,222 _____

9. Number Sense Melvin estimated
645 + 322 by adding 600 + 300. Is his
estimated sum an overestimate or an
underestimate? _____

Adding Whole Numbers and Money

You can add numbers by adding the ones, then tens, then hundreds, and then thousands. For example:

Adding Larger Numbers

Add 53,482 + 38,811.

Estimate: 50,000 + 40,000 = 90,000

Add each place from right to left.

```
  11 ─────────► Regroup the
  53,482        hundreds into
+ 38,811        1 thousand and
─────────       2 hundreds.
  92,293
```

The sum 92,293 is reasonable because it is close to the estimate of 90,000.

Adding Money

Add $88.50 + $11.75.

Estimate: $90 + $10 = $100

Add each place from right to left.

```
   11        Regroup as
$  88.50     necessary.
+  11.75
─────────
$100.25
```

Place the dollar sign and decimal point into the answer.

The sum $100.25 is reasonable because it is close to the estimate of $100.

Add.

1. 668
     + 343

2. $17.89
     +   2.71

3. 14,587
     + 5,532

4. 1,976
     +   240

5. $36.36
     + 24.84

6. 25,039
     + 37,949

7. $86.50
     +   5.65

8. 16,583
     + 83,795

9. Estimation Zach adds 4,731 and 1,150. Should his sum be more or less than 6,000?

_____

Column Addition

You can add more than two numbers when you line up the numbers by place value and add one place at a time.

Add 3,456 + 139 + 5,547.

Estimate: 3,000 + 100 + 6,000 = 9,100

Step 1	Step 2	Step 3
Line up numbers by place value. Add the ones. Regroup if needed.	Add the tens. Regroup if needed.	Add the hundreds, then the thousands. Continue to regroup.

Step 1

```
    2      22 becomes
3,456      2 tens and
  139      2 ones.
+ 5,547
─────────
    2
```

Step 2

```
   1 2
3,456
  139
+ 5,547
───────
   42
```
Keep digits in neat columns as you add.

Step 3

```
  1 1 2
3,456
  139
+ 5,547
───────
9,142
```
9,142 is close to the estimate of 9,100.

Add.

1.
```
   945
   124
+  343
```

2.
```
 2,588
   373
+  866
```

3.
```
12,566
 8,222
+ 5,532
```

4.
```
 2,955
 9,017
+  248
```

5.
```
$166.99
  33.11
+324.84
```

6.
```
$38.81
 17.35
+ 3.64
```

7. **Number Sense** Jill added 450 + 790 + 123 and got 1,163. Is this sum reasonable?

_____

_____

Name_____

Subtracting Whole Numbers and Money

Here is how to subtract across zeros.

Find 606 − 377.

Estimate: 600 − 400 = 200

Step 1	Step 2	Step 3	Step 4
606 − 377	5 10 6̶0̶6 − 377	9 5 10 16 6̶0̶6̶ − 377	9 5 10 16 6̶0̶6̶ − 377 ——— 229
You cannot subtract 7 ones from 6 ones, so you must regroup.	Since there is a zero in the tens place, you must regroup using the hundreds. Regroup 6 hundreds as 5 hundreds and 10 tens.	Regroup 10 tens and 6 ones as 9 tens and 16 ones.	Subtract. 1 1 229 + 377 ——— 606 You can check your answer by using addition.

Subtract.

1. $707
    −   58

2. 950
    − 47

3. 624
    − 379

4. $3,506
    −   866

5. $4,507
    − 3,569

6. 3,076
    − 1,466

7. $81.06
    − 29.99

8. 6,083
    − 1,492

9. **Reasonableness** Lexi subtracts 9,405 from 11,138. Should her answer be greater than or less than 2,000? Explain.

_____

_____

Choose a Computation Method

Use **mental math** when the problem is easy to do in your head.

Marlo needs to buy 10 bowls for the party. Each bowl costs $3. How much money will the 10 bowls cost?

$10 \times \$3 = \$30$
The total cost is $30.

Use **pencil and paper** when the problem does not have regroupings or is too difficult to solve mentally.

Mr. Davis has $45.55. He buys a baseball bat for $13.21. How much money does Mr. Davis have left?

$$\begin{array}{r} \$45.55 \\ -\ \ 13.21 \\ \hline \$32.34 \end{array}$$

Mr. Davis has $32.34 left.

Use a **calculator** for more complicated problems, like those that have a lot of regrouping. For example:

The Booster Club had a total of $1,080.50 in its account. Club members spent $179.05 on decorations for the school pep rally. How much money is left in the account?

Press:

1080.50   ⊟   179.05

  ⊟

Display: **901.45**

There is $901.45 left in the account.

Add or subtract.

1. $\begin{array}{r} 660 \\ -\ 360 \\ \hline \end{array}$

2. $\begin{array}{r} 3,546 \\ +\ \ \ 554 \\ \hline \end{array}$

3. $\begin{array}{r} 13,507 \\ -\ \ 8,569 \\ \hline \end{array}$

4. $\begin{array}{r} 1,276 \\ +\ 1,004 \\ \hline \end{array}$

5. **Number Sense** Explain why you would not use mental math to find $1,256 - 879$.

Name_____

Look for a Pattern

What pattern do you see?

    1 A 2 B 3 C 4 D 5 E 6 F

The numbers alternate with letters of the alphabet, in order.
The pattern would continue like this:

    7 G 8 H 9 I

What pattern do you see?

A	B	C
1	1	1
2	2	4
3	3	9
4	4	16
5		25

The number in column A is multiplied by the number in column B.
Column C is the product.

The last number in column B would be 5.

Look for a pattern. Draw the next two shapes.

1.

Look for a pattern. Write the three missing numbers.

2. 2, 4, 6, 8, _____ , _____ , _____

3. 2, 7, 12, 17, _____ , _____ , _____

4. 60, 52, 44, 36, _____ , _____ , _____

5. 88, 77, 66, 55, _____ , _____ , _____

PROBLEM-SOLVING SKILL   R 2-10

Translating Words to Expressions

A **number expression** contains numbers and at least one operation. Here are some examples:

67×3 $12 \div 4$ $67 + 89 + 13$ $177 - 54$

When you solve word problems, you use key words in the problem to make number expressions. For example:

> Kelly has 2 pencils. Juan has 3 more pencils than Kelly. How many pencils does Juan have?

Word phrase: more than

> *More than* refers to addition, so the number expression would be:
>
> $2 + 3$.

> Here are some other word phrases and the operations they refer to:

Word Phrase		Operation
more than total	plus combined with	addition
less than difference	fewer than minus	subtraction

Write a number expression for each phrase.

1. 37 marbles plus 52 marbles   _____

2. 30 days less than 365 days   _____

3. $45 increased by $67   _____

4. 25 tickets, with 18 tickets more   _____

5. Number Sense Jerry sees 15 bikes in the bike rack. He knows there are 35 total spaces for bikes. What operation can he use to find out how many more bikes will fit in the bike rack?

_____

Name

Matching Words and Number Expressions

Number expressions that require more than one operation use parentheses to indicate which operation should be done first.

Lori had 40 baseball cards. She gave 7 to Theo and 3 to Linda. How many cards did Lori have left?

Step 1: Write a number expression.
$40 - (7 + 3)$

Step 2: Find the value of the expression. Because this number expression has parentheses around $7 + 3$, you would do this part first.

$40 - (7 + 3)$
$\Downarrow$
$40 - 10 = 30$
Lori has 30 cards left.

Choose the number expression that matches the words. Then find its value.

1. Mr. Roundtree had 20 tickets. He gave 10 to his family and 8 to his friends.

   $20 - (10 - 8)$ or $(20 - 10) - 8$ _____

2. Jane made 8 hamburgers. She sold 6, but then made 2 more.

   $(8 - 6) + 2$ or $8 - (6 + 2)$ _____

3. Lonzo had 24 CDs. He lost 3 and gave 5 to a friend. How many CDs does Lonzo have?

   $(24 - 3) - 5$ or $24 - (3 - 5)$ _____

4. **Number Sense** Do $18 - (10 + 3)$ and $(18 - 10) + 3$ have the same value? Explain.

   _____

Evaluating Expressions

To evaluate an expression, replace the variable with a value
and then compute. For example:

Suppose $t = 5$. To evaluate $t + 20$,	$t + 20$
substitute 5 for t.	$\Downarrow$
Then add.	$5 + 20 = 25$

How can you find the missing number in this table?

n	$n + 11$	
5	16	$5 + 11 = 16$
8	19	$8 + 11 = 19$
10	21	
12		

Substitute 12 for n in the expression $n + 11$.
$12 + 11 = 23$. The missing number is 23.

Evaluate each expression for $a = 7$.

1. $a + 22 =$ _____   **2.** $a - 6 =$ _____   **3.** $17 + a =$ _____

4. Number Sense Does the expression
$f - 13$ have a greater value when $f = 23$
or when $f = 26$?   _____

Evaluate each expression for $n = 9$.

5. $n \div 3 =$ _____   **6.** $n + 15 =$ _____   **7.** $n - 7 =$ _____

Find the missing numbers in each table.

8.

n	$n - 5$
20	15
31	
50	45
17	

9.

$\star$	$\star + 21$
7	
9	30
30	51
40	

Solving Addition and Subtraction Equations

An equation is a number sentence stating that two expressions are equal.

$$7 + 5 = 12$$
$$12 = 12$$

Some equations have variables, such as $n + 20 = 100$. To solve the equation, you must find the number the variable stands for. Solve $n + 20 = 100$.

Step 1	Step 2
Use mental math. What number plus 20 equals 100?	See if the number works. If it doesn't, try another number.
Try different numbers.	Does $70 + 20 = 100$?
Try $n = 70$.	No.
$70 + 20 = 90$	Try $n = 80$.
	$80 + 20 = 100$
	So, $n = 80$.

Solve each equation.

1. $a + 5 = 12$ _____
2. $n + 9 = 18$ _____

3. $e - 6 = 60$ _____
4. $j + 100 = 126$ _____

5. $w - 200 = 100$ _____
6. $88 + t = 100$ _____

7. **Number Sense** Is the solution of $100 - f = 60$ greater than or less than 60? Explain how you know.

_____

_____

8. **Reasonableness** Marty solved the equation $d + 71 = 87$ and got $d = 12$. Is this solution reasonable? Explain.

_____

PROBLEM-SOLVING APPLICATIONS
These Lakes Are Great!

Suppose that waves in a part of Lake Michigan caused the water temperature to change quickly from 72°F to 59°F.

How many degrees cooler did the water temperature become?

To find the difference, subtract.

$$\begin{array}{r} \overset{6\ 12}{\cancel{7}\cancel{2}} \\ -\ 59 \\ \hline 13 \end{array}$$

So, the water temperature is 13°F cooler.

In its deepest part, Lake Michigan is about 925 ft deep.
The average depth of Lake Michigan is about 279 feet.

1. Find the difference between the depths.

_____

The shoreline of Lake Michigan is 1,638 miles. The shoreline of Lake Superior is 2,726 miles. The shoreline of Lake Erie is 871 miles.

2. How many miles of shoreline do the three lakes have combined?

_____

3. How many more miles of shoreline does Lake Michigan have than Lake Erie?

_____

4. Writing in Math Candice says that the shoreline of Lake Erie and Lake Michigan combined is greater than the shoreline of Lake Superior. Is she correct? Explain.

_____

_____

Name_____

Meanings for Multiplication

Addition sentence:

$5 + 5 + 5 + 5 = 20$

Multiplication sentence:

$4 \times 5 = 20$

There are 4 rows of 5.

There are 3 boxes. There are 7 books in each box.

Addition sentence:

$7 + 7 + 7 = 21$

Multiplication sentence:

$3 \times 7 = 21$

There are 3 groups of 7.

Write an addition sentence and a multiplication sentence for each picture.

1.

_____

2. ☆ ☆ ☆ ☆
☆ ☆ ☆ ☆
☆ ☆ ☆ ☆

_____

Write a multiplication sentence for each addition sentence.

3. $10 + 10 + 10 + 10 = 40$ _____

4. $3 + 3 + 3 + 3 + 3 + 3 = 18$ _____

5. Number Sense Explain how multiplication can help you find $7 + 7 + 7$.

_____

Patterns in Multiplying by 0, 1, 2, 5, and 9

Pattern	Example
All multiples of two are even numbers.	2, 18, 44
All multiples of 5 end in 0 or 5.	25, 100, 220
For all multiples of nine, the sum of the digits is always a multiple of 9.	27 $2 + 7 = 9$ 63 $6 + 3 = 9$
The product of any number and zero is zero.	$17 \times 0 = 0$
The product of any number and one is that number.	$32 \times 1 = 32$
Two numbers can be multiplied in any order and the product will be the same.	$4 \times 5 = 20$ $5 \times 4 = 20$

1. $\begin{array}{r} 9 \\ \times\ 5 \\ \hline \end{array}$

2. $\begin{array}{r} 2 \\ \times\ 8 \\ \hline \end{array}$

3. $\begin{array}{r} 8 \\ \times\ 5 \\ \hline \end{array}$

4. $\begin{array}{r} 9 \\ \times\ 0 \\ \hline \end{array}$

5. $\begin{array}{r} 9 \\ \times\ 3 \\ \hline \end{array}$

6. $\begin{array}{r} 7 \\ \times\ 2 \\ \hline \end{array}$

7. $\begin{array}{r} 0 \\ \times\ 3 \\ \hline \end{array}$

8. $\begin{array}{r} 1 \\ \times\ 56 \\ \hline \end{array}$

9. How many baseball cards are in 4 packages?

_____

Item	Number in Package
Baseball cards	5
Stickers	2
Coupon	1

10. How many stickers do you get if you buy 9 packages?

_____

11. How many coupons do you get if you buy 7 packages?

_____

Using Known Facts to Find Unknown Facts

You can use breaking apart to find a product.

Find 4 × 5.

4 groups of 5 are the same as 2 groups of 5 and 2 groups of 5.

 $2 \times 5 = 10$

$2 \times 5 = 10$

$4 \times 5 = 2 \times 5 + 2 \times 5$

$\quad\quad = 10 + 10$

$\quad\quad = 20$

Use breaking apart to find each product.

1.	3	**2.**	8	**3.**	4	**4.**	7
	× 5		× 3		× 9		× 7

5.	8	**6.**	8	**7.**	6	**8.**	4
	× 4		× 8		× 3		× 4

Compare. Use <, >, or = to fill in each ◯ .

9. $7 \times 6 \bigcirc 5 \times 7$

10. $9 \times 4 \bigcirc 4 \times 9$

11. $4 \times 4 \bigcirc 2 \times 8$

12. $7 \times 8 \bigcirc 9 \times 5$

Multiplying by 10, 11, and 12

Here are some easy ways to multiply numbers by 10, 11, and 12.

Multiples of 10

Any whole number multiplied by 10 will always equal that number with an additional zero in the ones place.

For example, $2 \times 10 = 20$, $22 \times 10 = 220$, and $220 \times 10 = 2,200$.

You can also break apart equations to help find products.

Multiples of 11

To find 12×11, think of 11 as $10 + 1$.

$12 \times 10 = 120$, $12 \times 1 = 12$, $120 + 12 = 132$, so $12 \times 11 = 132$.

Multiples of 12

To find 6×12, think of 12 as $10 + 2$.

$6 \times 10 = 60$, $6 \times 2 = 12$, $60 + 12 = 72$, so $6 \times 12 = 72$.

---

1. $5 \times 11 =$ _____
2. $12 \times 4 =$ _____
3. $10 \times 9 =$ _____

4. $7 \times 12 =$ _____
5. $12 \times 11 =$ _____
6. $8 \times 10 =$ _____

7. **Number Sense** Explain how 9×10 can help you find 9×11.

_____

There are 11 players on the field for each football team during a game. How many players would there be on

8. 4 teams? _____

9. 8 teams? _____

10. 10 teams? _____

11. 11 teams? _____

Name_____

Make a Table

Roller Blades Bill needs $119 to buy a new pair of roller
blades. He makes $15 a week delivering the Sunday paper. Will
Bill have the money he needs to buy the roller blades if he
saves his earnings for 8 weeks?

Read and Understand

Step 1: What do you know?

Bill makes $15 per week and needs $119 for new
roller blades.

Step 2: What are you trying to find?

Will he have enough money if he works for
8 weeks?

Plan and Solve

Step 3: What strategy will you use?   **Strategy:** Make a Table

Week	1	2	3	4	5	6	7	8
$ Saved	$15	$30	$45	$60	$75	$90	$105	$120

Yes, he will have enough money to buy the roller blades.

Look Back and Check

Step 4: Is your work correct?

Yes, the table shows that after 8 weeks he will have $120,
which is enough to buy the roller blades.

Vitamin Factory At a vitamin factory, 12 vitamins are formed
every 10 sec. How many vitamins will be formed in 60 sec?

1. Complete the table for the Vitamin Factory problem.

Seconds	10	20	30			
Vitamins	12	24				

Meanings for Division

When you divide, you separate things into equal groups.

Doris is making 8 box lunches, each with the same number of strawberries. She has a total of 32 strawberries. How many strawberries should go in each lunch?

What you think: Doris will have to place an equal number of strawberries in each box. She must put 32 strawberries into 8 equal groups. How many strawberries are in each group?

What you show: 8 equal groups

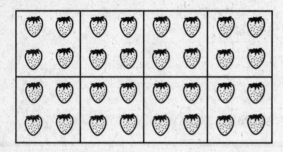

32 strawberries divided into 8 separate groups leaves 4 strawberries in each group.

What you write: $32 \div 8 = 4$

32 is the dividend, the number that is being divided.

8 is the divisor, the number the dividend is being divided by.

4 is the quotient, or the answer to the division problem.

Each lunch should have 4 strawberries.

Draw pictures to solve each problem.

1. You put 15 marbles into 3 groups.
    How many marbles are in each group?

    _____

2. You need to put 20 ice cubes into
    5 glasses. How many cubes
    should go in each glass?

    _____

Name_____

Relating Multiplication and Division

Multiplication and division are related, just like addition and subtraction are related.

This is the fact family for 5, 6, and 30:

$5 \times 6 = 30$ $\qquad$ $30 \div 6 = 5$

$6 \times 5 = 30$ $\qquad$ $30 \div 5 = 6$

Complete each fact family.

1. $2 \times$ _____ $= 10$ $\qquad$ $10 \div 5 =$ _____

_____ $\times$ _____ $= 10$ $\qquad$ $10 \div$ _____ $=$ _____

2. $9 \times$ _____ $= 27$ $\qquad$ $27 \div 3 =$ _____

_____ $\times$ _____ $= 27$ $\qquad$ $27 \div$ _____ $=$ _____

3. $8 \times$ _____ $= 72$ $\qquad$ $72 \div 8 =$ _____

_____ $\times$ _____ $= 72$ $\qquad$ $72 \div$ _____ $=$ _____

4. $6 \times$ _____ $= 48$ $\qquad$ $48 \div 8 =$ _____

_____ $\times$ _____ $= 48$ $\qquad$ $48 \div$ _____ $=$ _____

Write a fact family for each set of numbers.

5. 7, 4, 28 _____

_____

6. 5, 8, 40 _____

_____

7. **Number Sense** What multiplication facts are part of the fact family for $12 \div 3 = 4$?

_____

Division Facts

Thinking about multiplication facts can help when you want to divide. For example: Sunny and her father are packing oranges. They have 42 oranges. Each crate holds 6 oranges. How many crates do they need?

What You Think	**What You Say**	**What You Write**
What number times 6 = 42?	42 divided by 6 is what number?	$42 \div 6 = 7$
_____ $\times 6 = 42$	**or**	**or**
7 times 6 equals 42 $7 \times 6 = 42$	How many times does 6 go into 42?	$\begin{array}{r} 7 \\ 6\overline{)42} \end{array}$

---

1. $16 \div 2 =$ _____   **2.** $12 \div 4 =$ _____

3. $50 \div 5 =$ _____   **4.** $24 \div 8 =$ _____

5. $5\overline{)30}$ _____   **6.** $7\overline{)49}$ _____

7. $7\overline{)56}$ _____   **8.** $8\overline{)64}$ _____

9. Reasoning If $66 \div 6 = 11$, what is $66 \div 11$? Explain.

_____

_____

10. A ticket to ride the roller coaster costs $3. How many rides can you get for $15?   _____

11. Steve spends $24 on books. Books cost $8 each. How many books did Steve buy?   _____

Name_____

Special Quotients

There are special rules for dividing numbers by 1 and by 0.

Rule: A number divided by 1 is that number.

Examples: $4 \div 1 = 4$ $55 \div 1 = 55$

Rule: A number divided by itself (except 0) is 1.

Examples: $17 \div 17 = 1$ $135 \div 135 = 1$

Rule: Zero divided by a number (except 0) is 0.

Examples: $0 \div 4 = 0$ $0 \div 15 = 0$

Rule: You cannot divide a number by zero.

Examples: $7 \div 0$ cannot be done. $12 \div 0$ cannot be done.

1. $0 \div 2 =$ _____

2. $4 \div 4 =$ _____

3. $7\overline{)0}$ _____

4. $9\overline{)9}$ _____

5. $0 \div 3 =$ _____

6. $10\overline{)10}$ _____

7. $11\overline{)0}$ _____

8. $11 \div 1 =$ _____

Compare. Use >, <, or = for each $\bigcirc$.

9. $6 \div 6 \bigcirc 3 \div 3$

10. $7 \div 1 \bigcirc 8 \div 8$

11. $0 \div 5 \bigcirc 3 \div 1$

12. $0 \div 4 \bigcirc 0 \div 9$

13. $5 \div 5 \bigcirc 0 \div 5$

14. $7 \div 7 \bigcirc 9 \div 9$

15. $8 \div 1 \bigcirc 0 \div 8$

16. $9 \div 9 \bigcirc 9 \div 1$

17. $0 \div 12 \bigcirc 12 \div 1$

18. $0 \div 11 \bigcirc 0 \div 15$

19. **Number Sense** If $a \div b = 0$, what do you know about a? _____

Multiplication and Division Stories

Tile Floor Darren is laying a tile floor in the hallway. The pattern for the floor is shown to the right.

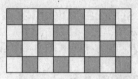

First, use Darren's tile floor to write a multiplication story for $4 \times 8 = 32$.

> Darren's tile floor has 4 rows with 8 pieces of tile in each row. How many pieces of tile are there in all?

Second, use Darren's tile floor to write a division story for $32 \div 4 = 8$.

> Darren has 32 small triangles. He needs 4 for each shaded square. How many shaded squares can he make with the small triangles?

Use the data in the table to write a multiplication or a division story for each number fact. Solve.

Building Supplies	Number in a Box
Fasteners	6
Bolts	12

1. 6×4

_____

_____

_____

2. $12 \div 4$

_____

_____

_____

PROBLEM-SOLVING SKILL

Multiple-Step Problems

Lawn Cutting Chad and his brother Brad cut lawns in their neighborhood to make money. They charge $20 per lawn. One weekend, Brad cut 4 lawns, and Chad cut 3 lawns. How much money did they earn altogether?

Solution One

Hidden Question: How many lawns did they mow altogether?

Chad cut 3 lawns, Brad cut 4 lawns.

$3 + 4 = 7$

They cut 7 lawns.

Question in the Problem: How much money did they earn altogether?

7 lawns $\times$ $20 = $140

Chad and Brad earned $140.

Solution Two

Hidden Question 1: How much money did Chad get for cutting lawns?

$3 \times $20 = $60

Hidden Question 2: How much money did Brad get for cutting lawns?

$4 \times $20 = $80

Question in the Problem: How much money did they earn altogether?

$60 + $80 = $140

Chad and Brad earned $140.

Write and answer the hidden question or questions. Then solve the problem. Write your answer in a complete sentence.

1. Keisha sold 8 ribbons. Then she sold 6 pins. The ribbons sold for $3; the pins sold for $2. How much money did Keisha make?

_____

_____

_____

_____

_____

_____

_____

Name_____

Writing and Evaluating Expressions

How to evaluate a multiplication expression:

Evaluate $5n$ for $n = 8$. Remember, $5n$ means the same as $5 \times n$.

First, substitute 8 for n. Then multiply.
$5 \times n = ?$
$5 \times 8 = ?$
$5 \times 8 = 40$

How to evaluate a division expression:

Evaluate $g \div 6$ for $g = 42$.

First, substitute 42 for g. Then divide.
$g \div 6 = ?$
$42 \div 6 = ?$
$42 \div 6 = 7$

How to evaluate expressions with more than one operation:

Evaluate $(4f) + 7$ for $f = 5$.

First, substitute 5 for f. Then do the computations inside the parentheses first.
$(4 \times f) + 7 = ?$
$(4 \times 5) + 7 = ?$
$20 + 7 = 27$

Evaluate each expression for $m = 4$.

1. $6m =$ _____

2. $\frac{m}{2} =$ _____

3. $20 \div m =$ _____

4. $(7m) + 2 =$ _____

5. Number Sense Write an expression that equals 50 for $n = 10$. _____

Evaluate each expression for $w = 7$.

6. $5 \times w =$ _____

7. $7 \div w =$ _____

8. $9w =$ _____

9. $3 \times (2 + w) =$ _____

Evaluate each expression.

10. $8 \times (4 + k)$ for $k = 2$ _____

11. $h \div (6 \times 1)$ for $h = 30$ _____

Name

Find a Rule

Complete the table. Start with the number in the **IN** column. What rule tells you how to find the number in the **OUT** column? Write the rule.

IN	OUT
2	10
4	20
6	30
8	
n	

What You Think

$2 \times 5 = 10$

$4 \times 5 = 20$

$6 \times 5 = 30$

$8 \times 5 = 40$

A rule is *multiply by 5*.

What You Write

IN	OUT
2	10
4	20
6	30
8	40
n	$n \times 5$

The rule *multiply by 5* is written as $n \times 5$.

Complete each table. Write the rule.

1.

In	20	25	35	55	n
Out	4	5	7		

2.

In	3	5	7	9	n
Out	9	15	21		

3.

In	2	5	7	10	n
Out	14	35	49		

Solving Multiplication and Division Equations

To solve an equation that has a variable you need to test several numbers for the variable. Find the one number that makes the equation true.

Solve the equation $4n = 28$ by testing these values for n: 5, 6, and 7.

Try	$n = 5$	$n = 6$	$n = 7$
Find 4n	$4 \times 5 = 20$	$4 \times 6 = 24$	$4 \times 7 = 28$
Does 4n = 28?	No	No	Yes

The solution to the equation is $n = 7$, because $4 \times 7 = 28$.

Solve the equation $g \div 5 = 9$ by testing these values for g: 30, 45, and 60.

Try	$g = 30$	$g = 45$	$g = 60$
Find g ÷ 5	$30 \div 5 = 6$	$45 \div 5 = 9$	$60 \div 5 = 12$
Does g ÷ 5 = 9?	No	Yes	No

The solution to the equation is $g = 45$, because $45 \div 5 = 9$.

Solve each equation by testing these values for k: 2, 4, and 6.

1. $k \div 2 = 3$ _____

2. $5k = 30$ _____

3. $36 \div k = 9$ _____

4. $8k = 16$ _____

Solve each equation by testing these values for n: 12, 16, and 24.

5. $n \div 6 = 4$ _____

6. $n \div 4 = 4$ _____

7. $n \times 2 = 24$ _____

8. $n \div 4 = 3$ _____

9. **Number Sense** What is the value of b in the equation $b \times 7 = 63$? How do you know?

_____

Name_____

The Party

Alberto is planning a party. He needs
to purchase the following items:

How much will Alberto have to spend
if he purchases 2 paper tablecloths?

$11 + $11 = $22

2 × $11 = $22

He will have to spend $22.

Party Supplies

Item	Price
Napkins	$2
Paper plates	$5
Cups	$9
Balloons	$10
Paper tablecloth	$11
Juice	$12

Use the chart above to answer the following questions.

1. Alberto purchased 6 packages of paper plates.
   The addition sentence that shows how much he
   spent is 5 + 5 + 5 + 5 + 5 + 5 = 30. Write the
   multiplication sentence for this addition sentence.

   _____

2. Since many people are coming to the party, Alberto
   purchased 9 packages of napkins. Complete the fact family.

   2 × _____ = 18   18 ÷ 9 = _____

   18 ÷ 2 = _____   _____ × _____ = 18

How much did Alberto spend on

3. 5 bottles of juice?   _____

4. 7 packages of cups?   _____

5. 4 packages of paper plates?   _____

6. Alberto spent $50 on balloons. How many
   bags of balloons did he purchase?   _____

Telling Time

You can read the time shown on the analog and digital clocks as either five forty or twenty minutes to six.

A.M. includes times from midnight until noon, and P.M. includes times from noon until midnight.

Write the time shown on each clock in two ways.

1. 10:40

2.

_____

_____

3. Write a reasonable time for leaving school. Include A.M. or P.M.

_____

4. **Reasoning** Would you most likely be asleep at 11:00 A.M. or 11:00 P.M.?

_____

Name_____

Units of Time

You can use the information in the table to compare different amounts of time. For example:

Which is longer, 3 years or
40 months?
According to the table,
1 year = 12 months.

Units of Time
1 minute = 60 seconds
1 hour = 60 minutes
1 day = 24 hours
1 week = 7 days
1 month = about 4 weeks
1 year = 52 weeks
1 year = 12 months
1 year = 365 days
1 leap year = 366 days
1 decade = 10 years
1 century = 100 years
1 millennium = 1,000 years

1 year = 12 months
3 years = 36 months

$$\begin{array}{r} 12 \\ \times\ 3 \\ \hline 36 \end{array}$$

40 months > 36 months
40 months > 3 years

So 40 months is longer
than 3 years.

Write <, >, or = for each ◯ .

1. 1 year ◯ 350 days

2. 25 months ◯ 2 years

3. 20 decades ◯ 2 centuries

4. 720 days ◯ 2 years

5. 8 decades ◯ 1 century

6. 72 hours ◯ 3 days

7. 240 minutes ◯ 3 hours

8. 3 years ◯ 120 months

9. **Number Sense** How many hours are in 2 days? _____

10. A score is 20 years. How many years is 5 score? _____

11. Dave's goldfish lived for 2 years, 8 months.
    Chris's goldfish lived for 35 months. Whose
    goldfish lived longer? _____

12. Tree A lived for 6 decades and 5 years. Tree B
    lived for 58 years. Which tree lived longer? _____

Name _____

Elapsed Time

Elapsed time problems can be solved in more than one way.

Find the elapsed time between 8:50 A.M. and 11:00 A.M.

One Way	**Another Way**
8:50 to 9:00 is 10 min	8:50 to 10:50 is 2 hr
9:00 to 11:00 is 2 hr	10:50 to 11:00 is 10 min
That's 2 hr and 10 min.	That's 2 hr and 10 min.

Find each elapsed time.

1. Start: 9:00 A.M.
   Finish: 1:30 P.M.   _____

2. Start: 5:15 P.M.
   Finish: 8:20 P.M.   _____

3. Start: 7:35 A.M.
   Finish: 8:57 A.M.   _____

Write the time each clock will show in 35 min.

4.

   _____

5.

   _____

6. **Number Sense** Is the elapsed time from 3:35 A.M. to 11:00 A.M. more than or less than 7 hr? Explain.

_____

_____

_____

Name_____

Writing to Compare

Football Practice

	Start Time	Water Break	Drills	End Time
Team A	3:00	3:45	4:00	5:00
Team B	3:30	4:00	4:05	5:15

Comparison Statements	Tips for Writing Good Comparisons
Team B starts practice 30 min later than Team A, but ends 15 min later. Team A gets a water break sooner than Team B, and the break is longer.	Use comparison words such as "later," "fewer," and "same."
Team A begins practice at 3:00 and ends at 5:00. That's 2 hr. Team B begins practice at 3:30 and ends at 5:15. That's 1 hr and 45 min. Team A has a longer practice.	Sometimes you can do calculations and compare the results.

1. In which corral does the cow roping last the longest?

_____

2. How long does the hog calling last in Corral No. 1?

_____

County Fair

Event		Corral No. 1	Corral No. 2
Bronco riding	Start	9:05	8:45
	End	10:15	10:05
Cow roping	Start	10:20	10:10
	End	11:35	11:15
Hog calling	Start	11:45	11:25
	End	1:10	1:05

3. In Corral No. 1, how much time is there from the start of the bronco riding to the end of the cow roping?

_____

Name_____

Calendars

Roberto is going on a business trip to Oregon on March 12.
He will be gone two weeks and one day. What date will he
return home?

March						
S	M	T	W	T	F	S
			1	2	3	4
5	6	7	8	9	10	11
12	13	14	15	16	17	18
19	20	21	22	23	24	25
26	27	28	29	30	31	

Move down two rows for two weeks and one column to the
right for one day. Roberto will return home on March 27.

Numbers such as twenty-seventh are called ordinal numbers.
They are used to tell order. Some other examples of ordinal
numbers are first, fourth, thirteenth, and seventy-first.

November						
S	M	T	W	T	F	S
			1	2	3	4
5	6	7	8	9	10	11
12	13	14	15	16	17	18
19	20	21	22	23	24	25
26	27	28	29	30		

December						
S	M	T	W	T	F	S
					1	2
3	4	5	6	7	8	9
10	11	12	13	14	15	16
17	18	19	20	21	22	23
24/31	25	26	27	28	29	30

Find the date

1. two weeks after November 7. _____

2. one week before November 13. _____

3. two weeks after December 7. _____

4. three weeks before December 26. _____

5. **Number Sense** How could you find the date
   two weeks after November 3, without a
   calendar? _____

6. Bill's birthday was three weeks before
   December 6. What date is Bill's birthday? _____

48 Use with Lesson 4-5.

Pictographs

A pictograph uses pictures or symbols to show data.

Endangered Species in the United States

Group	Number
Amphibians	🐾🐾🐾🐾🐾
Arachnids	🐾🐾🐾🐾🐾🐾
Crustaceans	🐾🐾🐾🐾🐾🐾🐾🐾🐾
Reptiles	🐾🐾🐾🐾🐾🐾🐾

Each 🐾 = 2 animals

Example

	How many types of arachnids are endangered?
What you think	Look next to Arachnids. There are 6 paws. Each 🐾 = 2 animals. 2, 4, 6, 8, 10, 12
What you write	There are 12 types of arachnids in the United States that are endangered.

Favorite Ways of Communicating with a Long-Distance Friend

E-mail	☺ ☺ ☺ ☾
Telephone	☺ ☺ ☺ ☺ ☺
Letters	☺ ☾

Each ☺ = 100 people

About how many people prefer to communicate by

1. e-mail? _____

2. telephone? _____

3. letter? _____

4. About how many more people prefer to use e-mail than letters?

   _____

5. **Number Sense** If each symbol on a pictograph equals 100 people, how many symbols would you need to show 750 people?

   _____

Line Plots

Line plots show data along a number line. Each X represents one number in the data.

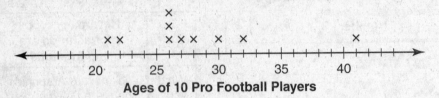

Ages of 10 Pro Football Players

Since there is one X above the 22, one of the pro football players is 22 years old.

Since there are three Xs above the 26, three of the pro football players are 26 years old.

The oldest player is 41 years old and the youngest player is 21.

The 41-year-old player is older than all of the other players. This number is called an outlier, since it is very different than the rest of the numbers.

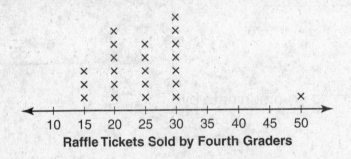

Raffle Tickets Sold by Fourth Graders

How many fourth graders sold

1. 15 raffle tickets?   _____

2. 20 raffle tickets?   _____

3. How many raffle tickets did most
   fourth graders sell?   _____

4. **Number Sense** Is there an outlier in the data set? Explain.

_____

_____

Bar Graphs

How to make a bar graph to display data

Data File

Lengths of U.S. States	
State	**Length**
Florida	500 mi
Georgia	300 mi
Kansas	400 mi
Utah	350 mi

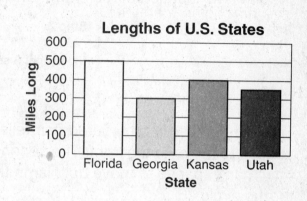

Step 1: Choose a scale.

Step 2: Draw and label the side and bottom of the graph.

Step 3: Draw a bar on the graph for each number in the data file.

Step 4: Give the graph a title. The title should be the subject of the graph.

---

1. Use the data at the right. Draw a bar graph with the number of points scored on the vertical axis and the players' names on the horizontal axis. Give the graph a title.

Player	Points Scored
Vito	30
Ray	25
Pat	35

Graphing Ordered Pairs

To name the location of the star on the grid:

Step 1:	**Step 2:**	**Step 3:**
Start at (0, 0).	Move right 3 spaces.	Move up 4 spaces.

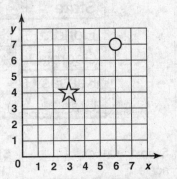

The star is located at (3, 4).

The first number in an ordered pair tells how many spaces to move to the right. The second number tells how many spaces to move up. Name the ordered pair for the circle. (6, 7)

An ordered pair names a point on a grid.

Name the ordered pair for each point.

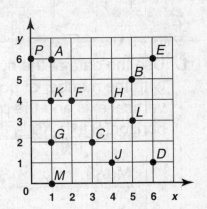

1. C _____

2. D _____

3. K _____

4. H _____

Give the letter of the point named by each ordered pair.

5. (5, 5) _____   **6.** (6, 6) _____   **7.** (2, 4) _____

Plot the following points on the coordinate grid below.

8. W(2, 4)

9. X(5, 6)

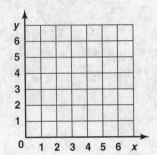

10. Y(3, 0)

11. Z(6, 1)

Line Graphs

Here is how to make a line graph.

Tomato Plant Growth

Day	Height (in cm)
5	5
10	7
15	10
20	20
25	30

Tomato Plant Growth

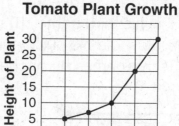

Step 1	Step 2	Step 3	Step 4
Choose an interval for each scale. Draw and label the side and bottom of the graph. Put time on the bottom.	Plot a point for each row in the data file. Plot (5, 5), (10, 7), and so on.	Draw a line from each point to the next one, in order.	Give the graph a title. The title should describe the subject of the graph.

Jones School Recycling

Month	Bins of Paper Recycled
1	5
2	15
3	35
4	40

1. The Jones School began a recycling program. After each month, students record how many bins of paper the school recycled. Draw a line graph that shows this data. Put the months of the school year at the bottom.

PROBLEM-SOLVING STRATEGY
Make a Graph

Pitcher Chris recorded 3 strikeouts in his first game, 5 in his second game, 7 in his third game, 10 in his fourth game, and 11 in his fifth game. How did his number of strikeouts change over the course of the five games he pitched?

Read and Understand

Step 1: What do you know?

I know the number of strikeouts Chris made each game.

Step 2: What are you trying to find?

How the number of strikeouts changed

Plan and Solve

Step 3: What strategy will you use?

A: Set up the bar graph.
B: Enter the known data.
C: Read the graph. Look for a pattern.

Answer: The number of strikeouts increased each game.

Strategy: Make a bar graph

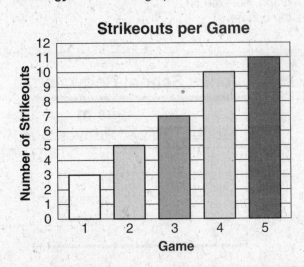

Solve. Write your answer in a complete sentence.

1. How much warmer is it, on average, in April than in January?

_____

_____

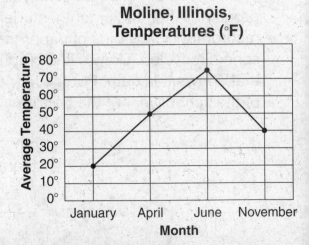

Median, Mode, and Range

You can summarize data by using median, mode, and range.

Data	Median	Mode	Range
	List the data in order from smallest to largest. Then find the number in the middle.	Find the number or numbers that occur most often. A set may have more than one mode.	Subtract the least number from the greatest number.
31, 32, 35, 40, 61, 61, 62	40 is the number in the middle. The median is 40.	61 is the number that occurs most often. 61 is the mode.	62 − 31 = 31 The range is 31.
25, 25, 26, 30, 47, 47, 48	The median is 30.	The modes are 25 and 47.	48 − 25 = 23 The range is 23.

Find the median, mode, and range of each set of data.

1. 8, 9, 3, 4, 6, 8, 7

_____

2. 8, 11, 10, 12, 15, 13, 10

_____

3. Reasoning Jill said the mode of the following set is 4. Is she correct? Explain. 1, 8, 7, 4, 2, 2

_____

_____

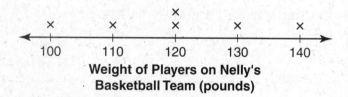

Weight of Players on Nelly's Basketball Team (pounds)

4. Find the mode, median, and range of the weights of the players on Nelly's basketball team.

_____

Data from Surveys

To take a survey, you ask different people the same question
and record their answers. Heather asked her class, "What is
your favorite flavor of frozen yogurt?" Here are her results:

Favorite Flavor of Frozen Yogurt

Vanilla	IIII	4
Chocolate	HHT IIII	9
Strawberry	III	3
Orange	I	1

We can see that Heather's classmates liked chocolate frozen
yogurt the best.

Favorite Winter Olympic Sports

Bobsledding	HHT III	
Curling	II	
Ice hockey	HHT HHT	
Speed skating	III	

1. How many people in the survey liked bobsledding
   the best? _____

2. How many people were surveyed? _____

3. According to the data, which sport is the favorite
   of most people? _____

4. **Number Sense** If five times as many people were
   surveyed, how many do you think would say they liked
   curling best? Explain.

   _____

   _____

   _____

Misleading Graphs

Sometimes graphs can be misleading. Make sure you always look at a graph closely.

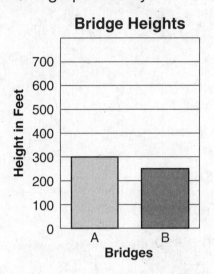

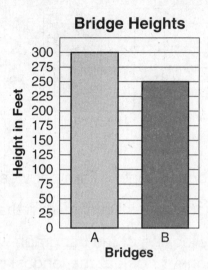

These graphs show the heights of two bridges. Look at the graph on the left. It looks as if the bridges are about the same height. However, when you look at the graph on the right, you see that Bridge A is 50 ft taller than Bridge B. The scale of the left graph is by 100s, while the scale of the right graph is by 25s.

---

1. Are there more students in the Math Club or in the Chemistry Club? Explain. How many students are in the Math Club? The Chemistry Club?

_____

_____

_____

After-School Clubs

_____

_____

2. **Reasoning** Is this graph misleading? Explain.

_____

Name_____

Time and Money

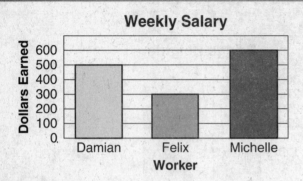

Weekly Salary

How much money does Michelle earn per week? $600

How much more money does Damian earn than Felix? $200

How can you tell by looking at the bar graph which person earned the most money? Look at the longest bar.

Clock A   Clock B

1. What time is shown on Clock A?   _____

2. What time is shown on Clock B?   _____

3. How much time has elapsed from Clock A to Clock B?

_____

Find the median, mode, and range of each set of data.

4. 17, 20, 22, 18, 19, 22, 24

_____

5. 105, 104, 104, 103, 106

_____

Multiplying by Multiples of 10, 100, or 1,000

Patterns can help you multiply by numbers that are multiples of 10, 100, or 1,000.

$3 \times 5 = 15$	$2 \times 4 = 8$	$5 \times 7 = 35$
$3 \times 50 = 150$	$2 \times 40 = 80$	$5 \times 70 = 350$
$3 \times 500 = 1,500$	$2 \times 400 = 800$	$5 \times 700 = 3,500$
$3 \times 5,000 = 15,000$	$2 \times 4,000 = 8,000$	$5 \times 7,000 = 35,000$

To find each of the products above, first complete the basic multiplication fact, then write the same number of zeros seen in the factor that is a multiple of 10. For example:

$3 \times 500 = 1,500$

First find 3×5. $3 \times 5 = 15$

Then, count the number of zeros
in the multiple of 10.   **500 has 2 zeros.**

Write 2 zeros to form the product.   **1,500**

Find each product. Use mental math.

1. $8 \times 80 =$ _____

2. $6 \times 60 =$ _____

3. $7 \times 90 =$ _____

4. $5 \times 200 =$ _____

5. $3 \times 400 =$ _____

6. $7 \times 200 =$ _____

7. $5,000 \times 6 =$ _____

8. $6,000 \times 9 =$ _____

9. $3 \times 8,000 =$ _____

10. $6,000 \times 7 =$ _____

11. Number Sense To find 8×600, multiply 8 and 6, then

write _____ zeros to form the product.

Name_____

Estimating Products

You can use rounding or compatible numbers to estimate products.

Estimate 7 × 28.

Using rounding numbers
Round 28 to 30.
7 × 30
7 × 30 = 210

Using compatible numbers
Replace 28 with 25.
7 × 25
7 × 25 = 175

Estimate each product.

1. 6 × 88 is close to 6 × _____

2. 59 × 4 is close to _____ × 4

3. 7 × 31   _____

4. 38 × 5   _____

5. 21 × 6   _____

6. 3 × 53   _____

7. 5 × 790   _____

8. 488 × 6   _____

9. Number Sense Estimate to tell if 5 × 68 is greater than or less than 350. Tell how you decided.

_____

_____

10. Estimate how many of Part C would be made in 4 months.

_____

11. Estimate how many of Part B would be made in 3 months.

_____

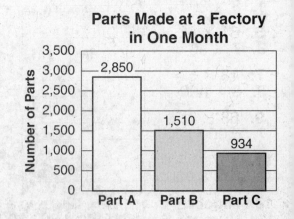

Parts Made at a Factory in One Month

12. Estimate how many of Part A would be made in 9 months.

_____

Mental Math

You can multiply mentally by breaking apart numbers or using compatible numbers.

Find 2 × 76 by breaking apart numbers.

Step 1: Use place value to break apart

76 into 70 and 6.

2 × 76

Step 2: Think of 2 × 76 as

2 × 70 and 2 × 6.

2 × 70 + 2 × 6

140 + 12

Step 3: Add the partial products to get the total.

140 + 12 = 152

2 × 76 = 152

Find 4 × 19 using compatible numbers.

Step 1: Substitute a compatible number for 19 that is easy to multiply by 4.

19 × 4
↓   Add 1 to make 20.
20 × 4

Step 2: Find the new product.

20 × 4 = 80

Step 3: Now adjust. Subtract 1 group of 4.
80 − 4 = 76.

4 × 19 = 76

Use mental math to find each product.

1. 5 × 32 = _____

2. 7 × 53 = _____

3. 66 × 2 = _____

4. 92 × 4 = _____

5. 31 × 82 = _____

6. 4 × 29 = _____

7. 18 × 5 = _____

8. 6 × 49 = _____

9. 68 × 3 = _____

10. 4 × 119 = _____

11. 107 × 5 = _____

12. 131 × 6 = _____

13. Algebra In $a \times b = 120$, a is a one-digit number and b is a two-digit number. What numbers could a and b represent?

_____

_____

Using Arrays to Multiply

You can use arrays of place-value blocks to multiply.

Find the product for 4 × 16.

What You Show	What You Write
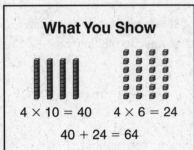 $4 \times 10 = 40$ $4 \times 6 = 24$ $40 + 24 = 64$	16 4 x 6 ones x 4 4 x 1 tens 24 40 64

Use the array to find the partial product and the product.
Complete the calculation.

1.
$$\begin{array}{r} 12 \\ \times \ \ 3 \\ \hline \end{array}$$

2.
$$\begin{array}{r} 22 \\ \times \ \ 6 \\ \hline \end{array}$$

3.
$$\begin{array}{r} 15 \\ \times \ \ 4 \\ \hline \end{array}$$

4.
$$\begin{array}{r} 22 \\ \times \ \ 4 \\ \hline \end{array}$$

5.
$$\begin{array}{r} 14 \\ \times \ \ 6 \\ \hline \end{array}$$

6.
$$\begin{array}{r} 16 \\ \times \ \ 6 \\ \hline \end{array}$$

7.
$$\begin{array}{r} 12 \\ \times \ \ 5 \\ \hline \end{array}$$

8.
$$\begin{array}{r} 13 \\ \times \ \ 4 \\ \hline \end{array}$$

9.
$$\begin{array}{r} 15 \\ \times \ \ 5 \\ \hline \end{array}$$

10.
$$\begin{array}{r} 16 \\ \times \ \ 7 \\ \hline \end{array}$$

11. **Number Sense** What two simpler problems can you use
to find 4 × 22? (Hint: Think about tens and ones.)

Multiplying Two-Digit and One-Digit Numbers

Here is how to multiply a two-digit number by a one-digit number using paper and pencil.

Find 3 × 24.	What You **Think**	What You **Write**
Step 1 Multiply the ones. Regroup if necessary.	$3 \times 4 = 12$ ones Regroup 12 ones as 1 ten 2 ones.	$\begin{array}{r} 1 \\ 24 \\ \times\ 3 \\ \hline 2 \end{array}$
Step 2 Multiply the tens. Add any extra tens.	3×2 tens $= 6$ tens 6 tens $+$ 1 ten $=$ 7 tens	$\begin{array}{r} 1 \\ 24 \\ \times\ 3 \\ \hline 72 \end{array}$

Is your answer reasonable?

Exact: $3 \times 24 = 72$

Round 24 to 20.

Estimate: $3 \times 20 = 60$ Since 72 is close to 60, the answer is reasonable.

Find each product. Decide if your answer is reasonable.

1. $\begin{array}{r} 13 \\ \times\ 3 \\ \hline \end{array}$
2. $\begin{array}{r} 17 \\ \times\ 7 \\ \hline \end{array}$
3. $\begin{array}{r} 24 \\ \times\ 5 \\ \hline \end{array}$
4. $\begin{array}{r} 48 \\ \times\ 8 \\ \hline \end{array}$

5. $\begin{array}{r} 62 \\ \times\ 6 \\ \hline \end{array}$
6. $\begin{array}{r} 36 \\ \times\ 5 \\ \hline \end{array}$
7. $\begin{array}{r} 88 \\ \times\ 5 \\ \hline \end{array}$
8. $\begin{array}{r} 52 \\ \times\ 8 \\ \hline \end{array}$

9. **Estimation** Use estimation to decide which has the greater product: 813×6 or 907×5. _____

Multiplying Three-Digit and One-Digit Numbers

Here is how to multiply larger numbers.

	Example A	Example B
Step 1 Multiply the ones. Regroup if necessary.	1 154 x 4 ____ 6	2 214 x 7 ____ 8
Step 2 Multiply the tens. Add any extra tens. Regroup if necessary.	2 1 154 x 4 ____ 16	2 214 x 7 ____ 98
Step 3 Multiply the hundreds. Add any extra hundreds.	2 1 154 x 4 ____ 616	2 214 x 7 ____ 1,498

Find each product. Estimate to check reasonableness.

1.	185 × 4	2.	517 × 4	3.	741 × 3	4.	413 × 6

5.	625 × 6	6.	381 × 5	7.	711 × 8	8.	802 × 5

9. **Number Sense** How could you use the product of 108 and 4 to find the product of 324 and 4?

10. A factory can make 241 footballs in 1 week. How many can it make in 9 weeks?

_____

Name_____

Try, Check, and Revise

Yard Sale Andrew spent $26 at his neighbor's yard sale. He bought three items. Which items did he buy?

Yard Sale	
Binoculars	$12
Shoehorn	$ 3
Bowling ball	$ 8
Army boots	$ 5
Slingshot	$ 6

Read and Understand

Step 1: What do you know?

He bought three items.
He spent $26.

Step 2: What are you trying to find?

Which three items did he buy?

Plan and Solve

Step 3: What strategy will you use?

Strategy: Try, check, and revise

Show the Main Idea

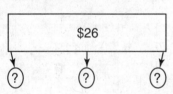

Try: The binoculars are $12. I'll try it plus two other items.

Check: Check using $12 + $8 + $5 = $25. That's too low.

Revise: I'll keep the binoculars and bowling ball, but try the slingshot instead of the army boots.

Use previous tries: $12 + $8 + $6 = $26 That's it!

Answer: He bought the binoculars, a bowling ball, and a slingshot.

Look Back and Check

Is your work correct?
Yes, the sum is $26, and he bought three items.

Use the first try to help you make a second try. Finish solving the problems.

1. Henry's dad bought 27 screws and nails at the hardware store. He bought twice as many screws as he did nails. How many of each did he buy? Try 8 screws.
   8 × 2 = 16 screws. 16 + 4 = 20. That's too low.

Name_____

Choose a Computation Method

When you compute, first try mental math.
Next, think about paper and pencil. For very
hard problems, use a calculator.

Cost of Summer Cottage Rental	
Cottage	Cost/Week
A	$ 595
B	$1,045
C	$1,887

Example A

What is the cost of a two-week stay at Cottage A?

$2 \times \$595 = ?$

This is easy to do in my head. I'll use mental math.

$2 \times 600 = 1,200$

$1,200 - 10 = 1,190$

Cost: $1,190

Example B

What is the cost of a three-week stay at Cottage B?

$3 \times \$1,045 = ?$

There are a lot of regroupings. I'll use paper and pencil.

$$\begin{array}{r} {\scriptstyle 1\ 1} \\ 1,045 \\ \times \quad\ 3 \\ \hline 3,135 \end{array}$$

Cost: $3,135

Example C

What is the cost of a seven-week stay at Cottage C?

$7 \times \$1,887 = ?$

There are a lot of regroupings. I'll use a calculator.

Press: 7   1887

Display: `13209`

Cost: $13,209

Find each product. Tell what computation method you used.

1. $\begin{array}{r} 4,100 \\ \times \quad\ 4 \\ \hline \end{array}$

2. $\begin{array}{r} 5,170 \\ \times \quad\ 4 \\ \hline \end{array}$

3. $\begin{array}{r} 1,857 \\ \times \quad\ 7 \\ \hline \end{array}$

4. $\begin{array}{r} 6,253 \\ \times \quad\ 6 \\ \hline \end{array}$

5. **Number Sense** Gary used paper and pencil to find $6,005 \times 4$.
Could he have found the answer a faster way? Explain.

_____

_____

_____

Multiplying Money

The steps for multiplying money are almost exactly the same as the steps for multiplying whole numbers.

For example, a meal deal at the local fast-food restaurant costs $4.89. How much would it cost to eat there 3 days in a row?

Step 1	**Step 2**
Multiply the same way as with whole numbers.	Write the answer in dollars and cents.

Step 1

Multiply the same way as with whole numbers.

$$\begin{array}{r} {\scriptstyle 2\ 2} \\ \$4.89 \\ \times \quad 3 \\ \hline 14\ 67 \end{array}$$

Step 2

Write the answer in dollars and cents.

$$\begin{array}{r} {\scriptstyle 2\ 2} \\ \$4.89 \\ \times \quad 3 \\ \hline \$14.67 \end{array}$$

Remember, there are two digits to the right of the decimal point when separating dollars and cents.

It costs $14.67 to eat there 3 days in a row.

Find each product.

1. $\begin{array}{r} \$1.21 \\ \times \quad 3 \\ \hline \end{array}$

2. $\begin{array}{r} \$3.15 \\ \times \quad 4 \\ \hline \end{array}$

3. $\begin{array}{r} \$7.23 \\ \times \quad 5 \\ \hline \end{array}$

4. $\begin{array}{r} \$4.18 \\ \times \quad 4 \\ \hline \end{array}$

5. $5.17 × 3 =$ _____

6. $70.14 × 3 =$ _____

7. $18.57 × 9 =$ _____

8. $62.53 × 4 =$ _____

9. **Estimation** If a salad costs $3.99, is $29.99 enough to buy 9 orders? Explain.

_____

Find each cost.

10. 3 boomerangs _____

11. 4 softballs _____

Item	Price
Boomerang	$6.49
Softball	$4.89

Multiplying Three Factors

You can use the Commutative and Associative Properties of Multiplication to make it easier to multiply 3 factors.

Commutative Property of Multiplication:

You can multiply any two numbers in any order.

$2 \times 3 = 3 \times 2$

Associative Property of Multiplication:

You can change the grouping of the factors.

$4 \times (2 \times 3) = (4 \times 2) \times 3$

Here are three ways to find $20 \times 2 \times 3$.

Example A	Example B	Example C
Multiply 20 and 2 first.	Multiply 2 and 3 first.	Multiply 20 and 3 first.
$20 \times 2 = 40$	$2 \times 3 = 6$	$20 \times 3 = 60$
$(20 \times 2) \times 3$	$20 \times (2 \times 3)$	$(20 \times 3) \times 2$
$40 \times 3 = 120$	$20 \times 6 = 120$	$60 \times 2 = 120$

1. $5 \times 3 \times 6 =$ _____

2. $50 \times 4 \times 2 =$ _____

3. $3 \times 30 \times 5 =$ _____

4. $4 \times 5 \times 60 =$ _____

5. $8 \times 2 \times 15 =$ _____

6. $6 \times 5 \times 10 =$ _____

7. $14 \times 2 \times 3 =$ _____

8. $50 \times 7 \times 5 =$ _____

9. **Number Sense** For $20 \times 5 \times 6$, is it easier to find 20×5 or 20×6 mentally? Why?

_____

_____

10. Show three ways to find $4 \times 25 \times 2$.

_____

Name_____

Choose an Operation

Understanding when to choose a particular operation can help
you solve problems.

READ AND UNDERSTAND **Show the main idea.**	The average male giraffe is 3 times taller than Ramon. Ramon is 6 feet tall. How tall is the average male giraffe? ☐ ☐ ☐ ☐ Ramon's Average height giraffe's height: 3 times as tall	A goldfish named Tish lived from 1956 to 1999. How many years did Tish live? 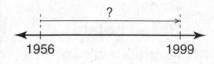
PLAN AND SOLVE **Choose an operation.**	Multiply to find "times as tall." 6 × 3 = 18 Ramon's Times Average height as giraffe's tall height	Subtract to compare the numbers. 1999 − 1956 = 43 Year Year Years in died born between

Draw a picture to show each main idea. Then choose an
operation and solve each problem.

1. If there are 4 qt of milk in 1 gal, and 2 pt in 1 qt, how many
    pints are in 5 gal?

_____

2. Runner A ran 844 mi last year. Runner B ran 1,063 mi. How
    many more miles did Runner B run than Runner A?

_____

Name_____

The Grocery Store

Caleb is preparing a meal for his friend. The chart shows the number of calories in each type of food.

Food	Amount	Grams	Calories
Seedless raisins	1 c	145	435
Salted butter	1 tbsp	14	100
Banana	1	114	105
Baked potato	1	156	145
Apple	1	138	80
Sardines	3 oz	85	175

Use mental math. How many calories are in:
    3 tbsp of salted butter? 300 calories
    4 apples? 320 calories

Use the chart above to answer the following questions.

1. How many calories are there
   in 7 baked potatoes?

2. How many calories are there
   in 8 c of seedless raisins?   _____

3. How many grams are there in
   6 oz of sardines?   _____

4. Use mental math to find out how many
   calories are in 4 bananas.   _____

Name _____

Multiplying Multiples of Ten

You can multiply with mental math by using basic facts and patterns.

Example A: $5 \times 5 = 25$

$5 \times 50 = 250$

$50 \times 50 = 2,500$

$50 \times 5,000 = 250,000$

The product contains the number of zeros in each factor.

Example B: $5 \times 6 = 30$

$5 \times 60 = 300$

$50 \times 60 = 3,000$

$50 \times 600 = 30,000$

$50 \times 6,000 = 300,000$

When the product of a basic fact includes a zero, such as $5 \times 6 = 30$, that zero is not part of the pattern.

Multiply. Use mental math.

1. $20 \times 20 =$

2. $50 \times 10 =$

3. $40 \times 40 =$

_____

_____

_____

4. $30 \times 80 =$

5. $60 \times 600 =$

6. $50 \times 900 =$

_____

_____

_____

7. $70 \times 3,000 =$

8. $70 \times 6,000 =$

9. $40 \times 5,000 =$

_____

_____

_____

10. Number Sense Tell what numbers go in the blanks.

To find 90×300, multiply _____ and _____.

Then write _____ zeros at the end.

Estimating Products

Estimate 11 × 94.

Using rounding	**Using compatible numbers**
Round 11 to 10.	Replace 11 with 10.
Round 94 to 90.	Replace 94 with 100.
10 × 90 = 900	10 × 100 = 1,000
11 × 94 is about 900 days.	11 × 94 is about 1,000.

To find the **range**, underestimate by replacing with lesser numbers or overestimate by replacing with greater numbers. In the above examples, 10 × 90 = 900 is an underestimate and 15 × 100 = 1,500 is an overestimate. So the range for these estimates is between 900 and 1,500.

Estimate each product.

1. 62 × 82

2. 59 × 48

3. 74 × 302

_____

4. 47 × 790

5. 498 × 63

6. 687 × 38

_____

Estimate each product by finding each range.

7. 32 × 83 _____

8. 37 × 22 _____

9. 51 × 296 _____

10. Number Sense To estimate the product of 37 × 99, Chris multiplied 40 × 100. Tell how you know if this is an underestimate or an overestimate.

_____

_____

Using Arrays to Multiply

Here is how to find the product of 12 × 24 using an array.

Draw a rectangle 24 units long by 12 units wide.

Divide the rectangle by tens and ones for each factor. Find the number of squares in each smaller square.

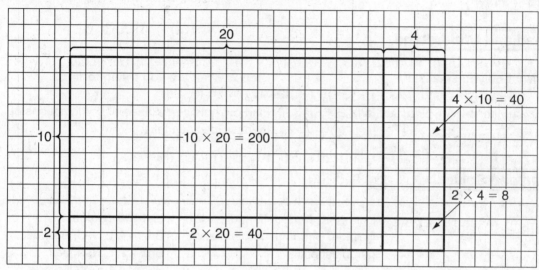

Then add the numbers of the squares in the four rectangles:

200 + 40 + 40 + 8 = 288

So, 12 × 24 = 288.

Divide the rectangle by tens and ones for each factor. Then complete the calculation.

1.

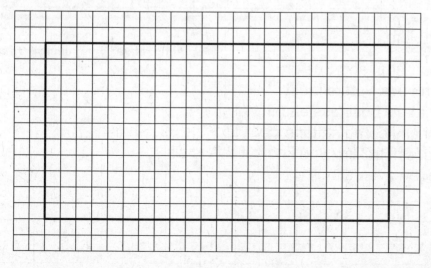

$$\begin{array}{r} 2\ 2 \\ \times\ 1\ 1 \\ \hline \end{array}$$

Name_____

Make an Organized List

Theme Park Brian has four passes to a theme park. He could bring himself and three friends. The group of friends for him to choose from includes Art, Ned, Jeff, and Belinda. How many different combinations are possible?

Read and Understand

Step 1: What do you know?

There are four friends: Art, Ned, Jeff, and Belinda.

Step 2: What are you trying to find?

Find out how many different combinations of friends Brian can take.

Plan and Solve

Step 3: What strategy will you use?

Strategy: Make an Organized List

Brian, Art, Ned, Jeff, and Belinda. Brian has to be in each combination.

List the choices:
Brian, Art, Ned, Belinda
Brian, Art, Ned, Jeff
Brian, Art, Jeff, Belinda
Brian, Ned, Jeff, Belinda

Answer: There are four combinations.

Look Back and Check

Is your work correct?

Yes, because each combination uses Brian. The way the list is organized shows that all ways were found.

Finish solving the problem.

1. Ann, Mara, Jenny, Tina, and Sue are sisters. Two of the five sisters must help their father at his business each Saturday. How many combinations of two sisters are possible?

| Ann | Mara | | Jenny | Tina |
| Ann | Jenny | | | |

_____

_____

Multiplying Two-Digit Numbers

There are 24 cars in the race. Each car has a 13-person crew in the pit area. How many pit-area workers are at the race?

Step 1	Step 2	Step 3
Multiply the ones. Regroup if necessary.	Multiply the tens. Regroup if necessary.	Add the partial products.

Step 1

Multiply the ones.
Regroup if necessary.

```
  1
  24
× 13
  72
```

Step 2

Multiply the tens.
Regroup if necessary.

```
  1
  24
× 13
  72
 240
```

Step 3

Add the partial products.

```
  1
  24
× 13
  72
 240
 312
```

24 × 13 = 312, so there are 312 pit-area workers at the race.

1.  ```
       38
    ×  26
    ```

2.  ```
       67
    ×  27
    ```

3.  ```
       44
    ×  85
    ```

4.  ```
       88
    ×  32
    ```

5. **Number Sense** Corina multiplied 62 × 22 and got a product of 1,042. Explain why Corina's answer is not reasonable.

_____

_____

_____

_____

_____

_____

Multiplying Greater Numbers

Multiply 626 × 47.

Step 1	Step 2	Step 3
Estimate: 600 × 50 = 30,000	Place a zero in the ones place.	Add the partial products.
Multiply the ones.	Multiply the tens.	
Regroup if necessary.	Regroup if necessary.	

Step 1

Estimate: 600 × 50 = 30,000

Multiply the ones.

Regroup if necessary.

$$
\begin{array}{r}
1\,4 \\
626 \\
\times\ 47 \\
\hline
4{,}382 \\
\end{array}
$$

Step 2

Place a zero in the ones place.

Multiply the tens.

Regroup if necessary.

$$
\begin{array}{r}
1\,2 \\
1\,4 \\
626 \\
\times\ 47 \\
\hline
4{,}382 \\
25{,}040 \\
\end{array}
$$

Step 3

Add the partial products.

$$
\begin{array}{r}
1\,2 \\
1\,4 \\
626 \\
\times\ 47 \\
\hline
4{,}382 \\
25{,}040 \\
\hline
29{,}422 \\
\end{array}
$$

The product 29,422 is reasonable, because it is a little less than the estimate of 30,000.

---

1. $\begin{array}{r} 113 \\ \times\ 26 \\ \hline \end{array}$

2. $\begin{array}{r} 517 \\ \times\ 44 \\ \hline \end{array}$

3. $\begin{array}{r} 741 \\ \times\ 43 \\ \hline \end{array}$

4. **Number Sense** Is 11,452 a reasonable answer for 28 × 409? Explain.

_____

_____

_____

Name_____

Choose a Computation Method

When you multiply, first try mental math. Next, think about
pencil and paper. For very hard problems, use a calculator.

Find 12 × $1,000.

This is easy to do, so you can
use mental math.

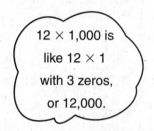

12 × 1,000 is
like 12 × 1
with 3 zeros,
or 12,000.

12 × $1,000 = $12,000

Find 810 × 15.

There are not a lot of
regroupings, so you can use
pencil and paper.

$$\begin{array}{r} 810 \\ \times\ 15 \\ \hline 4{,}050 \\ 8100 \\ \hline 12{,}150 \end{array}$$

810 × 15 = 12,150

Find 56 × 1,287.

There are a lot of regroupings,
so you can use a calculator.

Press: **56** ✕ **1287**

ENTER
=

Display: 72072

56 × 1,287 = 72,072

Multiply. Tell what method you used.

1. $\begin{array}{r} 400 \\ \times\ \ 40 \\ \hline \end{array}$ _____

2. $\begin{array}{r} 170 \\ \times\ \ 14 \\ \hline \end{array}$ _____

3. $\begin{array}{r} 784 \\ \times\ \ 33 \\ \hline \end{array}$ _____

4. Number Sense The heaviest car in the world weighs 7,353 lb. How much
would 12 of these cars weigh? What computation method did you use?

_____

Multiplying Money

The steps for multiplying money are almost exactly the same as the steps for multiplying whole numbers.

Find 16 × $7.89.

Step 1	Step 2	Step 3
Estimate: 16 × $7.89 ↓ ↓ 20 × $8 = $160 The product should be less than $160.	Multiply the ones and then multiply the tens. $$\begin{array}{r} 5\ 5 \\ \$7.89 \\ \times\quad 16 \\ \hline 47\ 34 \\ 78\ 90 \end{array}$$	Add the partial products. Place the dollar sign and decimal point in the answer. $$\begin{array}{r} 5\ 5 \\ \$7.89 \\ \times\quad 16 \\ \hline 47\ 34 \\ 78\ 90 \\ \hline \$126.24 \end{array}$$

The product $126.24 is reasonable, because it is less than the estimate of $160.00.

1. $4.68
    ×   14

2. $5.17
    ×   33

3. $9.14
    ×   23

4. $8.57
    ×   19

5. **Number Sense** Romario multiplies 18 × $5.35. Which of the following is most likely the product: $96.30, $9.60, or $960.30? Explain.

_____

_____

_____

PROBLEM-SOLVING SKILL
Writing to Explain

Here are some things you can do to write a good explanation in math.

Estimate the number of rectangles in all of the columns.

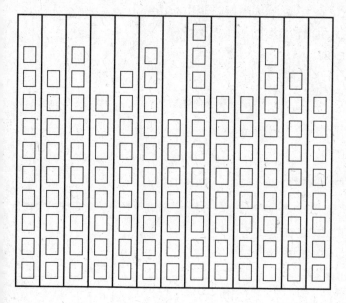

Show your computation clearly. Think about how you got your estimate. A flowchart can organize your thoughts. Write your steps in order.

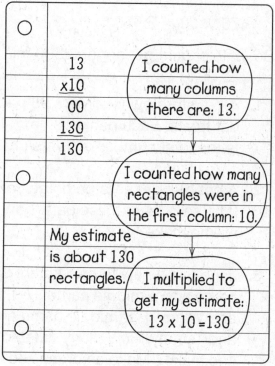

---

1. Use the pictograph to find out how many toy cars Andy has. Show your computation. You may use a flowchart to help show your thinking.

Toy Car Collection

Matthew	🚗 🚗 🚗
Andy	🚗 🚗 🚗 🚗 🚗
Ronald	🚗 🚗

Each 🚗 = 25 cars.

_____

_____

_____

Name_____

Cats

Cats are popular pets. Scientists estimate that there are over 100 million cats in the United States.

Cats should get about 70 min of exercise every week. Estimate how many minutes of exercise a cat should get in one year. Remember, there are 52 weeks in a year.

Use rounding:

$$70 \times 52$$
$$\downarrow \qquad \downarrow$$
$$70 \times 50 = 3{,}500$$

So, cats should get about 3,500 min of exercise each year.

---

1. A pet store owner orders 98 packages of cat treats. Each package has 115 treats. What is the total number of treats ordered?   _____

2. A cat breeder sells pedigree cats for $297. If he sells 24 of these cats, how much money will he make?   _____

3. Jane has a new female kitten. She wants to give it a first name and a middle name. Her first name choices are Fluffy and Wiggy. Her middle name choices are Margie, Carla, and Tammy. How many different name combinations can she make? Make an organized list to solve this problem.

_____

_____

_____

_____

_____

Using Patterns to Divide Mentally

When dividing numbers that end in zero, you can use basic division facts, as well as patterns, to help you divide mentally. For example:

	Find 210 ÷ 7.	Find 4,200 ÷ 6.
What You **Think**	First, find the basic fact. **210 ÷ 7 =** **21 ÷ 7 =** **21** tens **÷ 7 =** 3 tens or 30	Find the basic fact. **4,200 ÷ 6 =** **42 ÷ 6 =** **42** hundreds **÷ 6 =** 7 hundreds or 700
What You **Write**	210 ÷ 7 = 30	4,200 ÷ 6 = 700

Divide. Use mental math.

1. 250 ÷ 5 = _____

2. 7,200 ÷ 9 = _____

3. 200 ÷ 4 = _____

4. 28,000 ÷ 7 = _____

5. 810 ÷ 9 = _____

6. 50,000 ÷ 5 = _____

7. Number Sense What basic fact would you use to help solve 450,000 ÷ 9? _____

8. In 1 week there are 7 days. How many weeks are in 210 days? _____

9. How many weeks are there in 420 days? _____

Estimating Quotients

Estimate 460 ÷ 9.

You can use compatible numbers.

Ask yourself: What is a number close to 460 that could be easily divided by 9? Try 450.

450 ÷ 9 = 50

So, 460 ÷ 9 is about 50.

You can also estimate by thinking about multiplication.

Ask yourself: Nine times what number is about 460?

9 × 5 = 45, so 9 × 50 = 450.

So, 460 ÷ 9 is about 50.

50 is a good estimation for this problem.
Because 450 is less than 460, the estimated answer is an underestimate, that is, the actual answer is greater than 50.
An overestimate for this problem would be 540 ÷ 9 = 60.

Estimate each quotient. Tell whether you found an overestimate or an underestimate.

1. 165 ÷ 4   _____

2. 35 ÷ 4   _____

3. 715 ÷ 9   _____

4. 490 ÷ 8   _____

5. 512 ÷ 5   _____

6. 652 ÷ 8   _____

7. 790 ÷ 9   _____

8. 200 ÷ 7   _____

9. 311 ÷ 6   _____

10. Number Sense Find an overestimate and
     an underestimate for 313 ÷ 5.   _____

Dividing with Remainders

When you divide, you can think of putting items into groups.
For example:

$$60 \div 6 = 10$$

60 items   6 groups   10 items in
each group

Sometimes there are items left over. In division, the number of
"leftover" items is called the *remainder*. For example:

$$62 \div 6 = 10 \text{ R2} \longrightarrow 2 \text{ items}$$
left over

62 items   6 groups   10 items in
each group

Divide. You may use counters or pictures to help.

1. $4\overline{)34}$ **2.** $8\overline{)65}$ **3.** $9\overline{)75}$

4. $6\overline{)28}$ **5.** $5\overline{)14}$ **6.** $9\overline{)37}$

7. Number Sense In division, why should the remainder not
be greater than the divisor?

_____

Two-Digit Quotients

Here is how to divide two-digit quotients.

Find 37 ÷ 2.	What You **Show**	What You **Think**	What You **Write**
Step 1 Divide the tens.		There is 1 ten in each group and 1 ten left over.	$\begin{array}{r} 1 \\ 2\overline{)37} \\ -2 \\ \hline 1 \end{array}$
Step 2 Regroup by bringing down the ones.		Trade the extra ten for ten ones. The one ten and 7 ones make 17 ones.	$\begin{array}{r} 1 \\ 2\overline{)37} \\ -2 \\ \hline 17 \end{array}$
Step 3 Divide the ones.		There are 8 ones in each group and 1 one left over.	$\begin{array}{r} 18\,R1 \\ 2\overline{)37} \\ -2 \\ \hline 17 \\ -16 \\ \hline 1 \end{array}$

Use counters or draw pictures. Tell how many books are on each shelf and how many books are left over.

1. 66 books
   5 shelves _____

2. 78 books
   4 shelves _____

Divide. You may use counters or pictures to help.

3. $4\overline{)95}$

4. $2\overline{)57}$

5. $3\overline{)89}$

6. Number Sense You have 43 marbles. You divide them equally among some sacks. How many sacks must you use to get fewer than 8 marbles in each sack? _____

Name_____

Dividing Two-Digit Numbers

You can find two-digit quotients by breaking apart the problem
and dividing tens, then ones.

Find 85 ÷ 5.
Estimate: 100 ÷ 5 = 20.

```
        17
   5)85
     -5
      35
     -35
       0
```

Check: 17 × 5 = 85.
The answer checks.

Find 55 ÷ 3.
Estimate: 60 ÷ 3 = 20.

```
        18 R1
   3)55
     -3
      25
     -24
       1
```

Check: 18 × 3 = 54.
54 + 1 = 55
The answer checks.

Find 83 ÷ 7.
Estimate: 84 ÷ 7 = 12.

```
        11 R6
   7)83
     -7
      13
     - 7
       6
```

Check: 11 × 7 = 77.
77 + 6 = 83
The answer checks.

1.

```
      2 □
  3) 8 1
   -□
    □ 1
   -□□
      0
```

2.

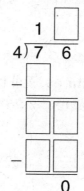

3. 3)91

4. 4)86

5. 2)75

PROBLEM-SOLVING SKILL

Interpreting Remainders

Muffins A parents' association was arranging muffins on plates for a bake sale. Each plate holds 6 muffins. There were 89 muffins baked for the sale.

When you solve a problem using division, the real-world situation tells you how to make sense of the remainder. For example:

Read and Understand	**Read and Understand**
How many plates will be filled?	How many muffins will be on the plate that is not filled?

Plan and Solve	**Plan and Solve**
Divide: $89 \div 6 = 14$ R5	Divide: $89 \div 6 = 14$ R5
The muffins will fill 14 plates.	There will be 5 muffins on the plate that is not filled.

Look Back and Check	**Look Back and Check**
14 plates will have 6 muffins each. There will be some muffins left over.	The remainder of 5 tells us that there are 5 extra muffins for another plate.

Solve.

The natural history museum has a hands-on mineral presentation. Each time the presentation is given, 8 students are permitted in the presentation area. One day, 100 students from Westbrook school were at the museum to see the presentation.

1. How many times must the presentation be given if all of the students see the presentation?

_____

2. How many groups of 8 will see the presentation?

_____

Name _____

Dividing Three-Digit Numbers

Find 454 ÷ 3.

Estimate: 450 ÷ 3 = 150.

Step 1	Step 2	Step 3	Check
Divide the hundreds.	Bring down the tens and divide.	Bring down the ones and divide.	Multiply the quotient by the divisor and add the remainder.

Step 1 — Divide the hundreds.

```
     1
3)454    Multiply.
 -3      Subtract.
  1      Compare.
         1 < 3
```

Step 2 — Bring down the tens and divide.

```
    15
3)454
 -3
  15     Multiply.
 -15     Subtract.
   0     Compare.
         0 < 3
```

Step 3 — Bring down the ones and divide.

```
   151 R1
3)454
 -3
  15
 -15
   04    Multiply.
 -  3    Subtract.
    1    Compare.
         1 < 3
```

Check — Multiply the quotient by the divisor and add the remainder.

```
    1
  151      453
 ×  3     +  1
  453      454
```

The answer checks.

1.

```
    [ ] 9 R[ ]
5) 3 4 9
 -[ ][ ]
   [ ][ ]
  -[ ][ ]
      [ ]
```

2.

```
    2 [ ] R[ ]
6) 1 6 9
 -[ ][ ]
   [ ][ ]
  -[ ][ ]
      [ ]
```

3. 7)378

4. 5)227

5. 6)513

6. Number Sense When looking at the divisor and the dividend, how can you tell where to begin dividing?

_____

_____

Zeros in the Quotient

Find 956 ÷ 9.

First estimate: 900 ÷ 9 = 100.

Step 1	Step 2	Step 3	Check
Divide the hundreds.	Bring down the tens and divide.	Bring down the ones and divide.	Multiply the quotient by the divisor and add the remainder.

Step 1

Divide the hundreds.

```
      1
  9)956    Multiply.
   -9
   ────
    0      Compare.
           0 < 9
```

Step 2

Bring down the tens and divide.

```
     10
  9)956
   -9
   ────
    05     Multiply.
   - 0     Subtract.
   ────
     5     Compare.
           5 < 9
```

5 can't be divided by 9. Place a zero in the quotient.

Step 3

Bring down the ones and divide.

```
    106 R2
  9)956
   -9
   ────
    05
   - 0
   ────
    56     Multiply.
   -54     Subtract.
   ────
     2     Compare.
           2 < 9
```

Check

Multiply the quotient by the divisor and add the remainder.

```
      5
    106        954
  ×   9      +   2
  ─────      ─────
    954        956
```

The answer checks.

Divide. Check your answer.

1. 7)742 **2.** 5)520 **3.** 2)813 **4.** 4)808

5. Number Sense Could 540 ÷ 3 be 18? Why or why not?

_____

_____

_____

_____

Dividing Money Amounts

Find $1.68 ÷ 3.

Estimate: $1.50 ÷ 3 = $0.50, so $1.68 ÷ 3 should be close to $0.50.

Step 1	Step 2	Check
Divide the same way you would with whole numbers.	Show the dollar sign and decimal point in the quotient. The decimal point should be moved straight up.	Multiply the quotient by the divisor.

Step 1

$$\begin{array}{r} 56 \\ 3)\overline{\$1.68} \\ -\underline{15} \\ 18 \\ -\underline{18} \\ 0 \end{array}$$

Step 2

$$\begin{array}{r} \$0.56 \\ 3)\overline{\$1.68} \\ -\underline{15} \\ 18 \\ -\underline{18} \\ 0 \end{array}$$

Check

$$\begin{array}{r} \$0.56 \\ \times \quad 3 \\ \hline \$1.68 \end{array}$$

The answer checks.

Divide. Check your answer.

1. 6)$3.12

2. 5)$5.35

3. 4)$8.80

4. 7)$4.55

5. Number Sense What is a good estimate for $4.21 ÷ 2?

_____

PROBLEM-SOLVING STRATEGY
Write a Number Sentence

The Painter Stephan spent $6.35 on paints for a painting on which he is working. He bought 5 tubes of paint. How much did each tube of paint cost?

Read and Understand

Step 1: What do you know? The 5 tubes of paint cost $6.35.

Step 2: What are you trying to find? How much each paint tube cost.

Plan and Solve

Step 3: What strategy will you use? Strategy: Write a number sentence.

Let t = cost of one tube of paint.

$6.35 \div 5 = t$

Solve for t.

```
       $1.27
    5)$6.35
      -5
      ‾‾‾
       13
      -10
      ‾‾‾
       35
      -35
      ‾‾‾
        0
```

So, each tube of paint costs $1.27.

Look Back and Check

Step 4: Is your answer reasonable? Yes, 5 × $1.27 = $6.35.

Solve the number sentence.

1. There are 364 students who will be taking a field trip. The students will ride on 7 buses. An equal number of students will ride on each bus. How many students will be on each bus?
    s = the number of students on each bus
    $364 \div 7 = s$ _____

Write a number sentence for the problem, then solve.

2. Sarah picked pears at her aunt's farm. She picked a total of 96 pears. She placed the pears into 8 baskets. How many pears did she place in each basket?

_____

_____

Divisibility Rules

You can use special rules to tell if a number is divisible by 2, 3, 5, 9, or 10.

A whole number is divisible by	Example
2 if the ones digit is even.	2, 16, 238
3 if the sum of the digits is divisible by 3.	324 $3 + 2 + 4 = 9$, $9 \div 3 = 3$
5 if the number ends in 0 or 5.	605, 310
9 if the sum of the digits is divisible by 9.	747 $7 + 4 + 7 = 18$, $18 \div 9 = 2$
10 if the number ends in 0.	60, 120, 350

Test each number to see if it is divisible by 2, 3, 5, 9, or 10.

1. 20 _____

2. 88 _____

3. 63 _____

4. 45 _____

5. 65 _____

6. 303 _____

7. 510 _____

8. 603 _____

9. 105 _____

10. 654 _____

11. Number Sense If a number is divisible by 10, is it always divisible by 2? Explain.

_____

_____

_____

_____

_____

Finding Averages

Follow these steps to find the average, or mean, of 13, 15, 14, and 18.

Step 1 Add the numbers: 13 + 15 + 14 + 18 = 60.	**Step 2** Count how many numbers are in the group. 4	**Step 3** Divide: 60 (the total of the numbers) ÷ 4 (how many numbers in the group) = 15 (the average, or mean, of the numbers)

Find the average, or mean, of each set of data.

1. 25, 13, 24, 34 _____

2. 16, 15, 17 _____

3. 7, 10, 9, 10 _____

4. 4, 7, 6, 7, 11 _____

5. 13, 17, 18, 20 _____

6. 30, 35, 39, 36 _____

7. **Number Sense** What are two numbers that have an average of 50?

_____

8. What was the average temperature of the four times shown in the chart? _____

Time	Temperature
9:00 A.M.	60°F
11:00 A.M.	62°F
1:00 P.M.	64°F
3:00 P.M.	74°F

Dividing by Multiples of 10

You can use basic facts to divide by multiples of 10.

There are rules for the number of zeros in the quotient.

Here are two examples:

$420 \div 70 =$	$400 \div 50 =$

What is the basic fact that will help solve this problem?
   $42 \div 7 = 6$
   Notice that there are no zeros in the numbers in the basic fact.
	What is the basic fact that will help solve this problem?
	   $40 \div 5 = 8$
	   In this case, there is a zero in the number 40 in the basic fact.

You can apply the following rule. the number of zeros in the quotient = the number of zeros in the divisor − the number of zeros in the dividend	You can apply the following rule. the number of zeros in the quotient = one less than the number of zeros in the divisor − the number of zeros in the dividend
So, $420 \div 70 = 6$.	So, $400 \div 50 = 8$.

Divide. Use mental math.

1. $80 \div 40 =$ _____

2. $810 \div 90 =$ _____

3. $2,400 \div 6 =$ _____

4. $2,500 \div 5 =$ _____

5. $210 \div 30 =$ _____

6. $1,200 \div 20 =$ _____

7. **Number Sense** What basic fact would you use to solve $4,500 \div 90$? _____

8. There are 540 students at Middlebury school. The students are arranged into 9 teams for a sports event. How many students are on each team?

_____

Dividing with Two-Digit Divisors

When you divide with a two-digit divisor, an estimate is an important first step.

Find 228 ÷ 24.

Step 1 Find a reasonable estimate. You can use compatible numbers or rounding to do so.

225 ÷ 25 = 9, so 9 is a good estimate.

Step 2 Divide using the estimate.

$$
\begin{array}{r}
9 \text{ R}12 \\
24\overline{)228} \\
-216 \\
\hline
12
\end{array}
$$

Step 3 Check your work.

$$
\begin{array}{r}
24 \\
\times\ 9 \\
\hline
216
\end{array}
\qquad
\begin{array}{r}
216 \\
+\ 12 \\
\hline
228
\end{array}
$$

The answer checks. 228 is the dividend.

Estimate each quotient. Then divide.

1. $12\overline{)264}$

2. $16\overline{)336}$

3. $45\overline{)810}$

4. $63\overline{)819}$

5. $21\overline{)672}$

6. $31\overline{)372}$

7. Number Sense What is a good estimate for 345 ÷ 26? _____

PROBLEM-SOLVING APPLICATION

The Appalachian Trail

Hiking Trip Lee and his family are planning a hiking trip on the Appalachian Trail. They are packing food in 3 lb bundles. How many bundles could they make with 51 lb of food?

What strategy can you use to solve this problem? Write a number sentence.

$51 \div 3 = b$. $b =$ the number of food bundles

```
     17
  3)51
  -3
   ‾‾
   21
  -21
   ‾‾
    0
```

They can pack 17 food bundles.

1. The Appalachian Trail goes through 14 states. There are about 78 mi of Appalachian Trail in Georgia, about 68 mi in New Jersey, and about 82 mi in Massachusetts. What is the average number of miles of trail in these 3 states?

   _____

2. There are about 560 mi of trail in Virginia. If a person planned to hike 8 mi per day, how many days would it take to hike the Virginia portion of the trail? Write a number sentence, then solve the problem.

   _____

   _____

3. Use divisibility rules to see if the total number of miles of Appalachian Trail (2,168 mi) is divisible by 2, 3, 5, 9, or 10.

   _____

   _____

Relating Solids and Plane Figures

Solid figures have three
dimensions: length, width,
and height. Many solids have
edges, faces, and vertices.

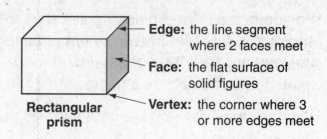

Edge: the line segment
where 2 faces meet

Face: the flat surface of
solid figures

Vertex: the corner where 3
or more edges meet

Rectangular
prism

Spheres, cylinders, and cones have curved surfaces.
Other solids have all flat surfaces.

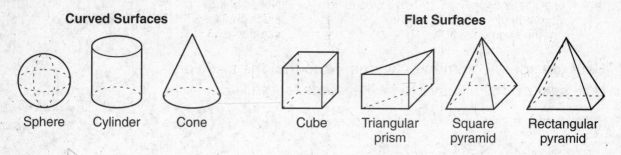

Curved Surfaces

Sphere   Cylinder   Cone

Flat Surfaces

Cube   Triangular
prism   Square
pyramid   Rectangular
pyramid

Complete the table.

	Number of Faces	Number of Edges	Number of Vertices	Shape(s) of Faces
Solid Figure				
1. Rectangular prism				
2. Cube				
3. Triangular prism				
4. Square pyramid				

5. **Reasoning** Compare rectangular pyramids and
rectangular prisms. How are they alike?

_____

_____

Polygons

Polygons are closed plane figures that are made up of line segments. All of the line segments connect. All of the sides of a polygon are straight, not curved.

Polygon
Closed figure made of line segments

Not a polygon
Not a closed figure

Not a polygon
Not all of the sides are line segments.

Here are some common polygons. Note that the sides of polygons do not all have to be the same length.

        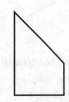

Octagon
8 sides

Hexagon
6 sides

Pentagon
5 sides

Quadrilateral
4 sides

Triangle
3 sides

Draw an example of each type of polygon.
How many sides and vertices does each
one have?

1. Hexagon

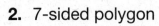
_____

2. 7-sided polygon

_____

3. Pentagon

_____

4. 9-sided polygon

_____

Lines, Line Segments, Rays, and Angles

Here are some important geometric terms.

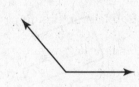

Line segment
A part of a line. It has two endpoints. This is line segment *XY*.

Ray
A part of a line. It has one endpoint and goes on and on in one direction. This is ray *AB*.

Right angle
A square corner.

Obtuse angle
Greater than a right angle.

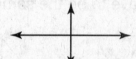

Parallel lines
Never intersect.

Intersecting lines
Pass through the same point.

Perpendicular lines
Lines that form right angles.

Use geometric terms to describe what is shown. Be as specific as possible.

1.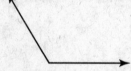

2.

3.

_____

_____

_____

_____

_____

_____

4. Name three different rays.

_____

5. Name two different line segments.

_____

Triangles and Quadrilaterals

Equilateral triangle
All sides are the same length.

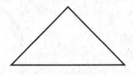

Isosceles triangle
At least two sides are the same length.

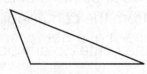

Scalene triangle
No sides are the same length.

Right triangle
One angle is a right angle.

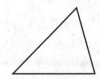

Acute triangle
All three angles are acute angles.

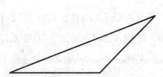

Obtuse triangle
One angle is an obtuse angle.

Square
There are four right angles. All sides are the same length.

Rectangle
There are four right angles.

Parallelogram
Opposite sides are parallel.

Rhombus
Opposite sides are parallel and all sides are the same length.

Trapezoid
There is only one pair of parallel sides.

Classify each triangle by its sides and then by its angles.

1.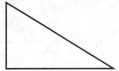

_____

2.

_____

Write the name of each quadrilateral.

3.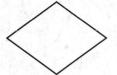

_____

4.

_____

Name_____

Circles

A circle is made up of all points that are
the same distance from the center point.

A radius connects the center to any point
on the circle.

A chord connects any two points on
the circle.

A diameter connects two points on the circle
and passes through the center of the circle.

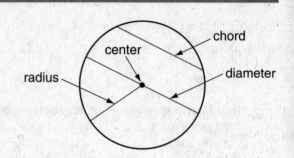

State whether the line segment shown is a radius, a chord, or a diameter.

1.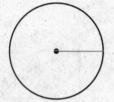

2.

3.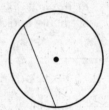

4.

_____   _____   _____   _____

5. **Writing in Math** How is a chord different from a radius?

_____

_____

_____

_____

For each circle shown, find the length of the diameter.

6.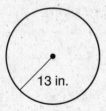
13 in.

7.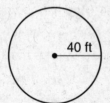
40 ft

8.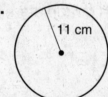
11 cm

9.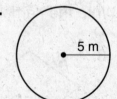
5 m

_____   _____   _____   _____

Congruent Figures and Motions

When two figures have the same shape and size, they are congruent.

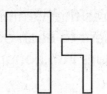

Not congruent
Different size.

Congruent
Same size and shape.

Not congruent
Different shape and size.

Figures can be moved in three ways: by slides, flips, or turns. When a figure is moved, its size and shape do not change.

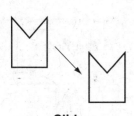

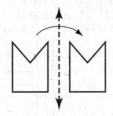

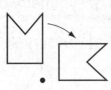

Slide
Moves the figure in a straight direction.

Flip
Gives the figure its mirror image. Sometimes the object looks the same after being flipped.

Turn
Moves a figure about a point.

Do the figures in each pair appear to be congruent? If so, tell if they are related by a flip, slide, or turn.

1.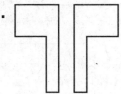

_____

_____

2.

_____

_____

3.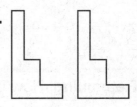

_____

_____

4. **Reasoning** Could the letters L and M ever be congruent? Explain.

_____

_____

Symmetry

Symmetric figures are figures that can be folded to make two halves that are congruent to each other. The lines that divide a symmetric figure into congruent halves are called lines of symmetry.

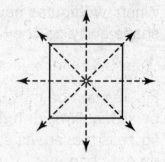

This square has 4 lines of symmetry. If you fold the square along any of the 4 dashed lines, the two halves will lie on top of each other.

How many lines of symmetry does each figure have?

1.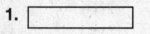

2.

3.

4.

_____   _____   _____   _____

5.

6.

7.

8.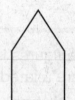

_____   _____   _____   _____

9. **Reasoning** How many lines of symmetry does the letter R have?   _____

10. Complete the drawing so that the figure is symmetric.

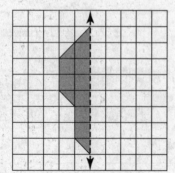

Name_____

Similar Figures

Similar figures are figures that have the same shape. The figures may or may not have the same size.

These triangles are about the same size, but they do not have the same shape. The triangles are NOT similar.

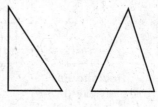

These shapes are similar. They have the same shape but are not the same size.

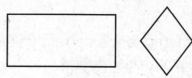

Do the figures in each pair appear to be similar? If so, are they also congruent?

1.

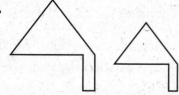

_____

2.

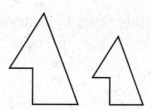

_____

3.

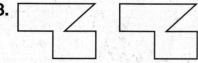

_____

4.

_____

5.

_____

6.

_____

Name _____

Writing to Describe

How would you describe the figures below?

 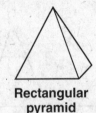 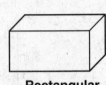

Cube   Rectangular   Rectangular
              pyramid   prism

Tips for writing a math description:

- Make a list of all the geometric terms that tell about or describe how the shapes are alike.

- Choose the terms to use in your answer.

- Use geometric terms correctly when you write your description.

Example

Geometric terms that describe how the shapes are alike:

> solid figures
>
> flat surfaces
>
> have rectangular faces

Since all of the shapes have height, width, and depth, they are all solid figures. They all have flat surfaces, and each of them has at least one rectangular face. They all have edges and vertices.

---

1. Write two statements to describe how the pairs of lines are alike.

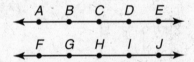

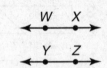

_____

_____

2. Write three statements comparing rectangular prisms and rectangular pyramids.

_____

_____

Perimeter

You can use addition to find the perimeter of a figure.

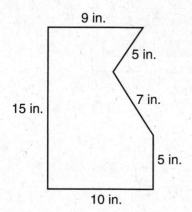

9 in.

5 in.

7 in.

15 in.

5 in.

10 in.

Add the lengths of the sides.

$9 + 5 + 7 + 5 + 10 + 15 = 51$ in.

Sometimes you can use a formula to find the perimeter.

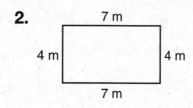

11 m

3 m   3 m

11 m

$P = 2l + 2w$

l is the length and w is the width.

$P = 2l + 2w$

$P = (2 \times 11) + (2 \times 3)$

$P = 22 + 6$

$P = 28$ m

Find the perimeter of each figure.

1.

8 cm

5 cm

8 cm

6 cm

3 cm

2 cm

_____

2.

7 m

4 m   4 m

7 m

_____

3.

7 in.

9 in.

4 in.

_____

4.

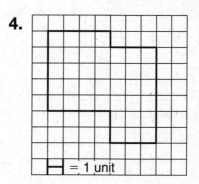

= 1 unit

_____

Name_____

Area

What is the area of this rectangle?

Use the formula $A = lw$:

$A = 8 \times 5$

$A = 40$

The area is 40 square feet.

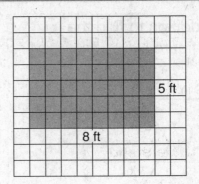

What is the area of this figure?

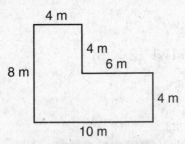

You can draw segments to divide the figure into rectangles. Then find the area of each rectangle and add.

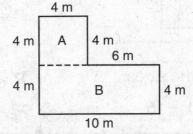

Rectangle A

$A = lw$

$A = 4 \times 4$

$= 16$

Rectangle B

$A = lw$

$A = 4 \times 10$

$= 40$

$16 + 40 = 56$, so the area of the original figure is 56 square meters.

Find the area of each rectangle.

1.

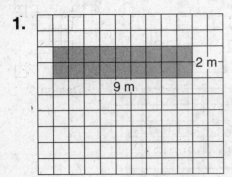

2.

_____   _____

3. Reasoning The area of a rectangle is 56 square inches. The width of the rectangle is 7 in. What is the length? _____

PROBLEM-SOLVING STRATEGY

Act It Out

The Paper Marla wants to buy a newspaper from a newspaper vending machine on the street corner. The vending machine takes only nickels and dimes. The cost of the paper is $0.75. What is the fewest number of coins Marla can use to buy the paper?

Read and Understand

Step 1: What do you know?

A paper costs $0.75. The vending machine takes only nickels and dimes.

Step 2: What are you trying to find?

Find the least number of coins Marla will need.

Plan and Solve

Step 3: What strategy will you use?

Strategy: Act it out

Use coins to act it out. Combine different numbers of nickels and dimes to make $0.75. One combination is 5 dimes and 5 nickels, a total of 10 coins. The best combination is 7 dimes and 1 nickel, a total of 8 coins.

Look Back and Check

Step 4: Is your work correct?

Yes. Any combination must have at least 1 nickel since the amount needed for the paper ends in 5.

---

1. How many squares are needed to make the 6th design?

   _____

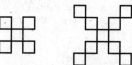 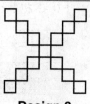

   Design 1   **Design 2**   **Design 3**

2. Tom and Toby each run every day. Tom runs 4 mi each day. Toby runs 5 mi every day. How many miles has Tom run when Toby has run 65 mi?

   _____

Volume

The number of cubic units needed to fill a solid figure is its volume. To find the volume of a solid figure, you can count each cube. The figure to the right has a volume of 8 cubic units.

You can also use multiplication to find the volume of a solid figure.

You can use the formula $V = lwh$.

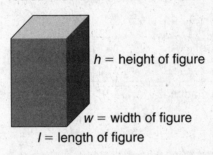

h = height of figure

w = width of figure

l = length of figure

Volume = length × width × height

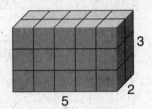

$V = lwh$
$V = 5 \times 2 \times 3$
$= 30$

The volume is 30 cubic units.

Find the volume of each figure.

1.

_____

2.

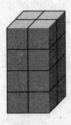

_____

3.

_____

4.

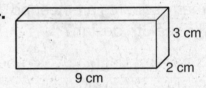

3 cm

2 cm

9 cm

_____

5. **Reasoning** A box with dimensions 4 in. by 4 in. by 4 in. is placed inside a box with dimensions 6 in. by 6 in. by 6 in. How much space is left inside the larger box after the smaller box is put inside?

_____

Name_____

The Living Room

Dana's parents are making some changes to their living room.
The east wall of the living room has two different paintings.

East Wall

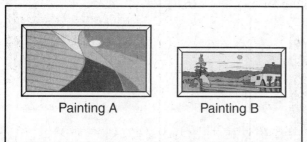

Painting A   Painting B

Are the paintings congruent?

No. They are the same shape but not the same size.

1. Dana's parents bought two round tables to be placed on each side of a couch. What is the diameter of Table X? What is the radius of Table Y?

   Table X
   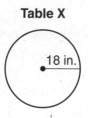
   18 in.

   Table Y
   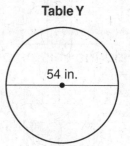
   54 in.

   _____

   _____

2. Are the tables similar, congruent, or both? Explain.

   _____

   _____

3. Dana's father thought it would be a good idea to move the living room rug. Was the rug moved by a slide, flip, or turn?

   _____

4. Dana's mother made a special design on the floor using tile. How many lines of symmetry does the design have?

   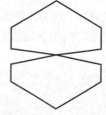

   _____

Parts of a Region

The top number, the numerator, tells the number of equal parts described. The bottom number, the denominator, tells how many equal parts there are in all.

$\dfrac{2}{3}$ ← Numerator. 2 parts are shaded.

$\phantom{\dfrac{2}{3}}$ ← Denominator. There are 3 parts total.

$\dfrac{2}{3}$ of the circle is shaded.

Write a fraction for the part of the region that is shaded.

1.

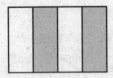

_____

2.

_____

3.

_____

4.

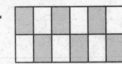

_____

Draw a model to show each fraction.

5. $\dfrac{5}{15}$

6. $\dfrac{7}{9}$

7. Reasoning Tara says that $\frac{1}{2}$ of a salad is always the same amount. Lynn says that it could be different amounts, depending on how large the salad is. Who is correct? Why?

_____

_____

_____

Parts of a Set

A fraction can describe a part of a set.

What fraction of each set is shaded?

There is a total of 5 squares. 3 of them are shaded. So, $\frac{3}{5}$ of the squares are shaded.

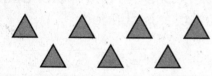

There is a total of 7 triangles. All 7 of them are shaded. So, $\frac{7}{7}$ of the triangles are shaded.

Draw a set with $\frac{3}{9}$ circles shaded.

The denominator tells how many circles are in the set, 9. So, draw 9 circles.

The numerator tells how many circles should be shaded, 3. So, shade in 3 circles.

What fraction of each set is shaded?

1. 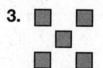   2.   3.   4.

_____ _____ _____ _____

Draw a picture to show each fraction as a part of a set.

5. $\frac{2}{9}$ 6. $\frac{4}{6}$

7. **Reasoning** Holly has a collection of 12 CDs. Of the 12 CDs, 7 of them are classical music. Write a fraction to show how many of the CDs are classical music.

_____

Fractions, Length, and the Number Line

How to show fractions on a number line:	How to write a fraction for the part of the length that is shaded:
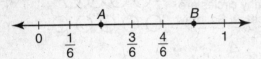	

The number line is divided into 6 equal lengths because the denominator is 6. The numerators go in order from 1 to 6. $\frac{2}{6}$ should be written at point *A*. $\frac{5}{6}$ should be written at point *B*.

The length has been divided into 9 equal parts. 9 is the denominator of the fraction. Because 5 of the lengths are shaded, 5 is the numerator of the fraction. So, $\frac{5}{9}$ is shaded.

Write a fraction for the part of each length that is shaded.

1. ├────────┼────────┼────────┤   _____

2. ├────────────┼──┼──┼──┤   _____

3. ├──┼──┼──┼──┼──┼──┼──┤   _____

4. ├────────┼────────────┤   _____

What fraction should be written at each point?

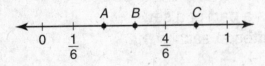

5. *A* _____   6. *B* _____   7. *C* _____

8. **Number Sense** To show $\frac{4}{5}$ on a number line, how many equal parts should be between 0 and 1? _____

Name_____

Estimating Fractional Parts

Benchmark fractions are fractions that are commonly used, such as $\frac{1}{4}$, $\frac{1}{3}$, $\frac{1}{2}$, $\frac{2}{3}$, and $\frac{3}{4}$. They are useful when you estimate fractional parts. For example:

About $\frac{1}{2}$ of the rectangle is shaded.

Point A is at about $\frac{1}{4}$.

Point B is at about $\frac{1}{2}$.

About $\frac{1}{3}$ of the length is shaded.

Estimate the fractional part of each that is shaded.

1.

_____

2. _____

_____

3.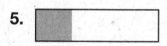

_____

4.

_____

5.

_____

6.

_____

Estimate the fraction that should be written at each point.

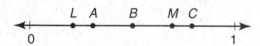

7. L _____

8. A _____

9. B _____

10. M _____

11. C _____

12. Number Sense There is a pan of food.
About $\frac{1}{4}$ of the food has been eaten.
About how much food is left?   _____

PROBLEM-SOLVING STRATEGY
Draw a Picture

The Fence A fence is 20 ft long. It has posts at each end and at every 4 ft along its length. How many fence posts are there?

Read and Understand

Step 1: What do you know?

The fence is 20 ft long.

There are fence posts at each end.

There are fence posts every 4 ft along the length of the fence.

Step 2: What are you trying to find?

How many posts the fence has

Plan and Solve

Step 3: What strategy will you use?

Strategy: Draw a picture

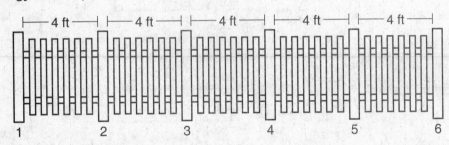

There are 6 fence posts altogether.

Look Back and Check

Step 4: Is your work correct?

Yes, the picture shows that there is a total of 6 fence posts.

Solve the problem. Write the answer in a complete sentence.

1. Tim, Kara, and Ann are working together to write a 4-page report. Each student is going to do an equal amount of writing. What fraction of the entire report does each student need to write?

Name_____

Equivalent Fractions

R 9-6

The fractions $\frac{3}{4}$ and $\frac{6}{8}$ both tell how much of the square is shaded. The fractions are equivalent.

You can find equivalent fractions using multiplication or division.

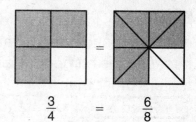

$$\frac{3}{4} = \frac{6}{8}$$

Using multiplication:

Write a fraction equivalent to $\frac{2}{7}$.

Multiply the numerator and denominator by the same number, but do not use zero.

$$\overset{\times\,3}{\underset{\times\,3}{\frac{2}{7} = \frac{6}{21}}}$$

So, $\frac{2}{7} = \frac{6}{21}$.

Using division:

Write a fraction equivalent to $\frac{8}{16}$.

Divide the numerator and denominator by the same number.

$$\overset{\div\,2}{\underset{\div\,2}{\frac{8}{16} = \frac{4}{8}}}$$

So, $\frac{8}{16} = \frac{4}{8}$.

Multiply or divide to find equivalent fractions.

1.
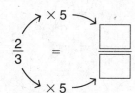

$$\overset{\times\,5}{\underset{\times\,5}{\frac{2}{3} = \frac{\boxed{}}{\boxed{}}}}$$

2.

$$\overset{\div\,2}{\underset{\div\,2}{\frac{6}{12} = \frac{\boxed{}}{\boxed{}}}}$$

3.
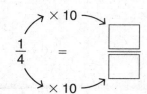

$$\overset{\times\,10}{\underset{\times\,10}{\frac{1}{4} = \frac{\boxed{}}{\boxed{}}}}$$

4.
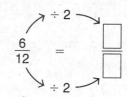

$$\overset{\div\,5}{\underset{\div\,5}{\frac{5}{20} = \frac{\boxed{}}{\boxed{}}}}$$

5. $\frac{4}{5}$ _____

6. $\frac{8}{10}$ _____

7. $\frac{7}{9}$ _____

8. $\frac{12}{16}$ _____

Use with Lesson 9-6. **115**

Fractions in Simplest Form

A fraction is in simplest form if the only common factor of the numerator and denominator is 1. $\frac{5}{20}$ in simplest form is $\frac{1}{4}$ because the numerator and denominator have no common factors other than 1.

Write $\frac{20}{30}$ in simplest form.

Step 1: Divide the numerator and denominator of the fraction by one of their common factors.

A common factor of 20 and 30 is 2.

$20 \div 2 = 10$

$30 \div 2 = 15$

Step 2: Check to see if $\frac{10}{15}$ is in simplest form.

No, 10 and 15 have a common factor of 5.

Repeat division.

Step 3: Divide the numerator and denominator by the common factor.

$10 \div 5 = 2$

$15 \div 5 = 3$

Step 4: Check to see if $\frac{2}{3}$ is in simplest form.

Yes, the only common factor of 2 and 3 is 1.

So, $\frac{20}{30}$ in simplest form is $\frac{2}{3}$.

Write each fraction in simplest form. If it is in simplest form, write *simplest form*.

1. $\frac{6}{8}$ _____

2. $\frac{9}{10}$ _____

3. $\frac{10}{12}$ _____

4. $\frac{7}{8}$ _____

5. $\frac{25}{50}$ _____

6. $\frac{3}{15}$ _____

7. $\frac{15}{22}$ _____

8. $\frac{16}{20}$ _____

9. **Writing in Math** Kevin said that $\frac{300}{500}$ is in simplest form because 3 and 5 have only 1 as a common factor. Is he correct? Explain why or why not.

_____

_____

_____

Using Number Sense to Compare Fractions

Leanne wanted to compare $\frac{4}{6}$ and $\frac{3}{4}$. She used fraction strips to help.

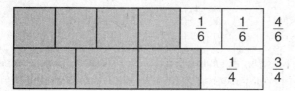

She compared the amounts that were shaded in each picture. Because the amount shaded in $\frac{3}{4}$ is more than the amount shaded in $\frac{4}{6}$, she knew that $\frac{3}{4}$ is greater than $\frac{4}{6}$.

So, $\frac{3}{4} > \frac{4}{6}$.

Write > or < for each $\bigcirc$. You may use fraction strips to help.

1. $\frac{5}{6}$ $\bigcirc$ $\frac{2}{3}$

2. $\frac{1}{5}$ $\bigcirc$ $\frac{2}{8}$

3. $\frac{9}{10}$ $\bigcirc$ $\frac{6}{8}$

4. $\frac{3}{4}$ $\bigcirc$ $\frac{1}{4}$

5. $\frac{8}{9}$ $\bigcirc$ $\frac{5}{10}$

6. $\frac{2}{5}$ $\bigcirc$ $\frac{2}{6}$

7. $\frac{6}{9}$ $\bigcirc$ $\frac{7}{9}$

8. $\frac{2}{10}$ $\bigcirc$ $\frac{3}{5}$

The same number of students attended school all week.

Day	Fraction of Students Buying Lunch
Monday	$\frac{1}{2}$
Tuesday	$\frac{2}{5}$
Wednesday	$\frac{3}{4}$
Thursday	$\frac{5}{8}$
Friday	$\frac{4}{6}$

9. Did more students buy lunch on Tuesday or on Wednesday? _____

10. Did more students buy lunch on Thursday or on Friday? _____

Comparing and Ordering Fractions

Comparing fractions:

Compare $\frac{1}{4}$ and $\frac{3}{8}$.

Multiply or divide to make the denominators the same. Then compare the numerators.

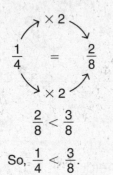

$$\frac{2}{8} < \frac{3}{8}$$

So, $\frac{1}{4} < \frac{3}{8}$.

Ordering fractions: Order $\frac{1}{2}$, $\frac{1}{4}$, and $\frac{3}{8}$ from least to greatest.

Use equivalent fractions.

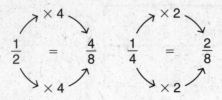

Compare the numerators. $\frac{2}{8} < \frac{3}{8}$ and $\frac{3}{8} < \frac{4}{8}$

The fractions in order are: $\frac{1}{4}$, $\frac{3}{8}$, $\frac{1}{2}$

Compare. Write >, <, or =.

1. $\frac{1}{6}$ ◯ $\frac{2}{8}$

2. $\frac{3}{5}$ ◯ $\frac{3}{10}$

3. $\frac{5}{7}$ ◯ $\frac{6}{9}$

4. $\frac{1}{2}$ ◯ $\frac{4}{6}$

Order the numbers from least to greatest.

5. $\frac{1}{2}$, $\frac{1}{3}$, $\frac{1}{4}$ _____

6. $\frac{2}{3}$, $\frac{3}{4}$, $\frac{2}{5}$ _____

7. $\frac{2}{9}$, $\frac{4}{5}$, $\frac{2}{8}$ _____

8. $\frac{1}{4}$, $\frac{7}{8}$, $\frac{5}{6}$ _____

9. **Writing in Math** Orlando wrote that $\frac{4}{5}$ is less than $\frac{4}{6}$. Is he correct? If not, explain how to find the correct answer.

_____

_____

_____

_____

Mixed Numbers and Improper Fractions

How to write mixed numbers as improper fractions:

Write $3\frac{1}{5}$ as an improper fraction.

First multiply the denominator by the whole number.

$3\frac{1}{5}$ $5 \times 3 = 15$

Add the numerator to this sum. $15 + 1 = 16$

Write the sum as the numerator. ⟶ $\frac{16}{5}$

Use the denominator from the fraction. ⟶

So, $3\frac{1}{5} = \frac{16}{5}$.

How to write improper fractions as mixed numbers:

Write $\frac{7}{4}$ as a mixed number.

First divide the numerator by the denominator.

$$4\overline{)7}$$
$$-\underline{4}$$
$$3$$
$$\frac{1}{}$$

The quotient is the whole number.

The remainder is the new numerator.

The denominator stays the same.

$1\frac{3}{4}$

So, $\frac{7}{4} = 1\frac{3}{4}$.

Write each mixed number as an improper fraction.

1. $2\frac{1}{3}$ _____

2. $4\frac{1}{5}$ _____

3. $2\frac{3}{4}$ _____

4. $5\frac{2}{6}$ _____

Write each improper fraction as a mixed number or a whole number.

5. $\frac{13}{12}$ _____

6. $\frac{50}{10}$ _____

7. $\frac{23}{10}$ _____

8. $\frac{17}{15}$ _____

9. Writing in Math Is $\frac{45}{5}$ equal to a whole number or a mixed number? Explain how you know.

_____

_____

_____

_____

Comparing Mixed Numbers

Here are some ways to compare mixed numbers.

Compare $1\frac{4}{8}$ and $3\frac{1}{5}$.

You can look at the whole numbers to decide which mixed number is larger.

$3 > 1$, so $3\frac{1}{5} > 1\frac{4}{8}$.

Compare $2\frac{1}{4}$ and $2\frac{6}{8}$.

Use a number line.

$2\frac{2}{8} \quad 2\frac{4}{8} \quad 2\frac{6}{8}$

$2 \quad 2\frac{1}{4} \quad 2\frac{2}{4} \quad 2\frac{3}{4} \quad 3$

Because $2\frac{6}{8}$ is to the right of $2\frac{1}{4}$, it is greater.

So, $2\frac{6}{8} > 2\frac{1}{4}$.

Compare $1\frac{2}{7}$ and $1\frac{9}{14}$.

Find fractions with the same denominators.

$\times 2$

$1\frac{2}{7} = 1\frac{4}{14}$

$\times 2$

$1\frac{9}{14} > 1\frac{4}{14}$

So, $1\frac{9}{14} > 1\frac{2}{7}$.

Compare. Write $<$, $>$, or $=$ for each $\bigcirc$.

1. $3\frac{3}{4} \bigcirc 3\frac{5}{6}$

2. $1\frac{7}{8} \bigcirc 2\frac{7}{8}$

3. $2\frac{1}{2} \bigcirc 2\frac{2}{5}$

4. $5\frac{1}{5} \bigcirc 5\frac{2}{8}$

5. $5\frac{5}{25} \bigcirc 5\frac{4}{20}$

6. $6\frac{9}{10} \bigcirc 5\frac{8}{50}$

A large snowstorm hit northern New York in November, 2000. The table shows the number of feet of recorded snowfall in some areas during the storm.

Location	Feet of Snow
Central Buffalo	$1\frac{5}{6}$
Jamestown	$1\frac{1}{2}$
Buffalo	$2\frac{1}{12}$
West Monroe	$2\frac{1}{6}$

7. Which town got more snow, Jamestown or Central Buffalo?

_____

8. Which town got more snow, Buffalo or West Monroe?

_____

Circle Graphs

This circle graph shows what sport fourth-grade students liked best. $\frac{1}{2}$ of the students liked football the best. You know this because $\frac{1}{2}$ of the circle is shaded for football.

Because $\frac{1}{4}$ of the students liked soccer the best, $\frac{1}{4}$ of the circle is shaded for soccer. $\frac{1}{8}$ of the students liked hockey the best, and $\frac{1}{8}$ liked tennis the best.

Favorite Sports of Fourth Graders

For 1–5, use the circle graphs below.

2002 Winter Olympics Medals, Italy

2002 Winter Olympics Medals, China

1. What fraction of the medals won by Italy was gold?

   _____

2. What fraction of the medals won by China was silver?

   _____

3. What fraction describes the number of silver medals won by Italy?

   _____

4. What fraction describes the number of bronze medals won by China?

   _____

5. **Number Sense** Did China win more gold or bronze medals?

   _____

PROBLEM-SOLVING SKILL

Writing to Explain

Pasta Gina and her brother Don made homemade pasta with their mother. Gina made $3\frac{1}{4}$ pans of pasta. Don made $3\frac{3}{8}$ pans. Which person made more pasta?

Writing a Good Math Explanation

- Write your explanation in steps to make it clear.

- Tell what the numbers mean in your explanation.

- Tell why you took certain steps.

Example

- First I compared the whole numbers. Because they were the same, I knew I had to compare the fractions.

- Because $\frac{1}{4}$ and $\frac{3}{8}$ have different denominators, I multiplied the numerator and denominator of $\frac{1}{4}$ by 2 to get $\frac{2}{8}$.

- Then I could compare the mixed numbers $3\frac{2}{8}$ and $3\frac{3}{8}$. Because $3\frac{3}{8}$ is greater than $3\frac{2}{8}$, I knew that Don made more pasta.

1. Humans usually have 20 baby teeth, which are replaced by 32 adult teeth. Raul said he has lost $\frac{6}{20}$ of his baby teeth. Write two fractions equivalent to this number. Explain how you came up with the fractions.

_____

_____

_____

_____

_____

_____

Name_____

The Football Team

In a football game, there are a total of 22 players on the field at a time. One team plays offense and the other plays defense. What fraction of the players is on offense?

Offensive players ⟶ o o o o o o o o o o o

Defensive players ⟶ d d d d d d d d d d d

Because there are 22 players total, the denominator is 22. Because 11 of the players are on offense, the numerator is 11. So, $\frac{11}{22}$ players are on offense. In simplest form, $\frac{11}{22} = \frac{1}{2}$. So, $\frac{1}{2}$ of the players are on offense and $\frac{1}{2}$ are on defense.

1. The coaches made the players run sprints down the football field to get in shape. The running backs had to run down the field $6\frac{3}{4}$ times. The linemen had to run down the field $6\frac{5}{8}$ times. Which group ran more? Explain.

   _____

   _____

2. Because it was going to rain, the team covered the playing field with a tarp to keep it dry. About how much of the field has been covered with the tarp? _____

3. What fraction of players have their helmets on?

   _____

4. The team played 16 games during the season. They won 4 games. So, the fraction that shows the number of games they won is $\frac{4}{16}$. Write this fraction in simplest form.

   _____

Estimating Fraction Sums

When you add two fractions, the sum is going to be less than, equal to, or greater than 1. An easy way to estimate the sum is to compare both of the fractions to $\frac{1}{2}$.

If both of the fractions are less than $\frac{1}{2}$, then the sum is going to be less than 1.

Example: $\frac{1}{5} + \frac{1}{3} < 1$

If both of the fractions are greater than $\frac{1}{2}$, then the sum is going to be greater than 1.

Example: $\frac{4}{5} + \frac{6}{7} > 1$

To compare a fraction to $\frac{1}{2}$, divide the denominator by 2. If the numerator is less than your quotient, the fraction is less than $\frac{1}{2}$. If it is greater than your quotient, the fraction is greater than $\frac{1}{2}$.

Write $>$ or $<$ for each $\bigcirc$.

1. $\frac{3}{4} + \frac{5}{6} \bigcirc 1$　　2. $\frac{2}{7} + \frac{1}{3} \bigcirc 1$　　3. $\frac{5}{16} + \frac{3}{10} \bigcirc 1$　　4. $\frac{3}{12} + \frac{2}{12} \bigcirc 1$

5. $\frac{4}{5} + \frac{5}{7} \bigcirc 1$　　6. $\frac{6}{10} + \frac{9}{10} \bigcirc 1$　　7. $\frac{1}{3} + \frac{1}{4} \bigcirc 1$　　8. $\frac{2}{3} + \frac{7}{12} \bigcirc 1$

Estimate to decide whether each sum is greater than 1 or less than 1. If you cannot tell, explain why.

9. $\frac{9}{12} + \frac{2}{5}$　_____

_____

10. $\frac{1}{4} + \frac{7}{16}$　_____

11. **Number Sense** Is $\frac{2}{4} + \frac{8}{16}$ greater than, equal to, or less than 1? Explain.

_____

_____

_____

Adding Fractions with Like Denominators

How to add fractions that have the same denominator:

$\frac{2}{3} + \frac{2}{3}$

Step 1

Estimate.

$\frac{2}{3} > \frac{1}{2}$, so $\frac{2}{3} + \frac{2}{3} > 1$.

Step 2

Add the numerators. Keep the denominator the same. Write the sum of the numerators over the denominator.

$\frac{2}{3} + \frac{2}{3} = \frac{4}{3}$

Step 3

Simplify, if necessary.

$\frac{4}{3} = 1\frac{1}{3}$

So, $\frac{2}{3} + \frac{2}{3} = 1\frac{1}{3}$

The answer is reasonable since

$1\frac{1}{3} > 1$.

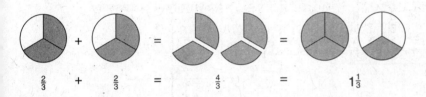

$\frac{2}{3}$ + $\frac{2}{3}$ = $\frac{4}{3}$ = $1\frac{1}{3}$

Find each sum.

1. $\frac{2}{5} + \frac{1}{5} =$ _____

2. $\frac{1}{3} + \frac{1}{3} =$ _____

3. $\frac{2}{4} + \frac{3}{4} =$ _____

4. $\frac{6}{10} + \frac{2}{10} =$ _____

5. $\frac{1}{5} + \frac{3}{5} =$ _____

6. $\frac{9}{16} + \frac{3}{16} =$ _____

7. $\frac{4}{12} + \frac{9}{12} =$ _____

8. $\frac{6}{7} + \frac{6}{7} =$ _____

9. $\frac{3}{15} + \frac{5}{15} =$ _____

10. $\frac{5}{10} + \frac{9}{10} =$ _____

11. Number Sense Jake estimates that $\frac{12}{19} + \frac{18}{19}$ is less than 1, since both fractions are less than 1. Is he correct?

_____

_____

_____

Adding Fractions with Unlike Denominators

To change fractions to like denominators, you write equivalent fractions.

Example: $\frac{1}{8} \times \frac{2}{2} = \frac{2}{16}$

So, $\frac{1}{8} = \frac{2}{16}$.

$$\begin{array}{r} \frac{2}{6} \\ + \frac{1}{4} \\ \hline \end{array}$$

Step 1	**Step 2**	**Step 3**
First estimate.	Find equivalent fractions with like denominators.	Add the numerators. Write the sum over the denominator. Simplify, if necessary.
$\frac{2}{6} < \frac{1}{2}$ and $\frac{1}{4} < \frac{1}{2}$, so $\frac{2}{6} + \frac{1}{4} < 1.$	$\begin{array}{r} \frac{2}{6} = \frac{8}{24} \\ + \frac{1}{4} = \frac{6}{24} \\ \hline \end{array}$	$\begin{array}{r} \frac{8}{24} \\ + \frac{6}{24} \\ \hline \frac{14}{24} = \frac{7}{12} \end{array}$ The sum is reasonable since $\frac{7}{12} < 1.$

1. $\begin{array}{r} \frac{5}{6} \\ + \frac{1}{3} \\ \hline \end{array}$

2. $\begin{array}{r} \frac{1}{4} \\ + \frac{4}{5} \\ \hline \end{array}$

3. $\begin{array}{r} \frac{3}{10} \\ + \frac{1}{20} \\ \hline \end{array}$

4. $\begin{array}{r} \frac{3}{4} \\ + \frac{1}{6} \\ \hline \end{array}$

5. $\begin{array}{r} \frac{1}{2} \\ + \frac{3}{8} \\ \hline \end{array}$

6. $\begin{array}{r} \frac{1}{9} \\ + \frac{2}{3} \\ \hline \end{array}$

7. **Reasoning** Carl says that since the sum of 3 and 5 is 8, he can use 8 as a denominator to add $\frac{1}{3} + \frac{1}{5}$. Is he correct? Explain.

_____

_____

Name_____

Subtracting Fractions with Like Denominators

When two fractions with the same denominator are being subtracted, the denominator in the difference remains the same and the numerators are subtracted.

Find $\frac{9}{12} - \frac{3}{12}$.

Step 1

Subtract the numerators. Write the difference over the denominator.

$$\frac{9}{12} - \frac{3}{12} = \frac{6}{12}$$

Note that the denominator stays the same.

Step 2

Simplify, if necessary.

$\frac{6}{12}$ is not in simplest form.

6 is a common factor of 6 and 12, so divide each number by 6.

$$\frac{6 \div 6}{12 \div 6} = \frac{1}{2}$$

So, $\frac{9}{12} - \frac{3}{12} = \frac{1}{2}$

---

1. $\frac{3}{5} - \frac{1}{5} = $ _____

2. $\frac{5}{9} - \frac{2}{9} = $ _____

3. $\frac{6}{12} - \frac{5}{12} = $ _____

4. $\frac{2}{3} - \frac{1}{3} = $ _____

5. $\begin{array}{r} \frac{4}{8} \\ - \frac{1}{8} \\ \hline \end{array}$

6. $\begin{array}{r} \frac{4}{7} \\ - \frac{3}{7} \\ \hline \end{array}$

7. $\begin{array}{r} \frac{7}{8} \\ - \frac{1}{8} \\ \hline \end{array}$

8. $\begin{array}{r} \frac{9}{12} \\ - \frac{1}{12} \\ \hline \end{array}$

9. **Estimation** Is $\frac{5}{8} - \frac{3}{8}$ more or less than $\frac{1}{2}$? Explain.

_____

_____

_____

_____

_____

Subtracting Fractions with Unlike Denominators

When the denominators are not easily found for both of the fractions, you can multiply the denominators together.

$$\frac{3}{7}$$
$$-\frac{1}{6}$$

Take the denominator from the second fraction, and multiply both the numerator and the denominator of the first fraction.

$$\frac{3 \times 6}{7 \times 6} = \frac{18}{42}$$
$$\frac{1}{6}$$

Take the denominator from the first fraction, and multiply both the numerator and the denominator of the second fraction.

$$\frac{3}{7} = \frac{18}{42}$$
$$-\frac{1 \times 7}{6 \times 7} = -\frac{7}{42}$$

After the fractions have like denominators, subtract the numerators. Simplify the answer if necessary.

$$\frac{3}{7} = \frac{18}{42}$$
$$-\frac{1}{6} = \frac{7}{42}$$
$$18 - 7 = \frac{11}{42}$$

1. $\frac{3}{4} - \frac{5}{8} =$ _____

2. $\frac{7}{10} - \frac{1}{2} =$ _____

3. $\frac{7}{8} - \frac{2}{16} =$ _____

4. $\frac{3}{5} - \frac{3}{10} =$ _____

5.
$$\frac{5}{6}$$
$$-\frac{3}{4}$$

6.
$$\frac{2}{3}$$
$$-\frac{1}{2}$$

7.
$$\frac{4}{7}$$
$$-\frac{3}{14}$$

8.
$$\frac{5}{6}$$
$$-\frac{7}{10}$$

9. **Number Sense** Simon ran $\frac{3}{4}$ of a mile on Monday, $\frac{1}{3}$ of a mile on Tuesday, and $\frac{1}{2}$ a mile on Wednesday. How much farther did Simon run on Monday than on Wednesday?

_____

PROBLEM-SOLVING STRATEGY

Use Logical Reasoning

Sports Alan, Jack, Todd, and Trent play baseball, basketball, football, and soccer. Alan does not play a sport that begins with the letter b. Todd plays football. Jack does not play basketball. What sport does Trent play?

Read and Understand

Step 1: What do you know?

Alan does not play baseball or basketball. Todd plays football. Jack does not play basketball.

Step 2: What are you trying to find?

What sport Trent plays

Plan and Solve

Step 3: What strategy will you use?

You know that Todd is playing football, so you then know that Alan, Jack, and Trent do not play football. You also know that Todd is not playing baseball, basketball, or soccer.

Answer: Trent plays basketball.

Strategy: Use logical reasoning

	Baseball	Basketball	Football	Soccer
Alan	No	No	No	Yes
Jack	Yes	No	No	No
Todd	No	No	Yes	No
Trent	No	Yes	No	No

Look Back and Check

Step 4: Is your work correct? Yes, I filled in the information I was given and made the right conclusions.

---

1. Joleen, Cori, and Bethany are cousins, but they each have a different last name. None of the cousins have a last name that begins with the same letter as their first name. Bethany is not a Carson. What is each cousin's full name?

	Butcher	Carson	Jacobson
Bethany			
Cori			
Joleen			

Name_____

Length and Customary Units

Unit	Example
inch	width of a U.S. quarter
1 foot (ft) = 12 inches (in.)	gym shoes
1 yard (yd) = 3 feet	height of a desk
1 mile (mi) = 5,280 feet	distance between school and home

How to measure an object:

To measure an object, make sure one end of the object begins at the zero unit.

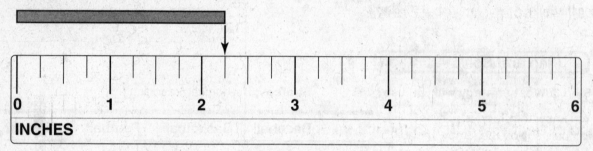

The rectangle is closest to the 2 in. mark, so we can say the rectangle is 2 in. long to the nearest inch.

Estimate first. Then find each length to the nearest inch.

1. |————————————————————| _____

2. |————————| _____

Choose the most appropriate unit to measure the length of each. Write in., ft, yd, or mi.

3. cat   _____   4. lake   _____

5. hallway   _____   6. basketball court   _____

Fractions of an Inch

The nail is just over $2\frac{1}{8}$ in. long.

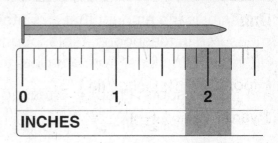

To the nearest inch, the nail is 2 in.

To the nearest $\frac{1}{2}$ in., the nail is also
2 in. long, because it is closer to 2 in.
than it is to $2\frac{1}{2}$ in.

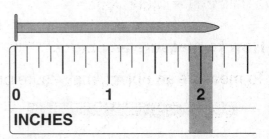

To the nearest $\frac{1}{4}$ in., the nail is $2\frac{1}{4}$ in. long,
because the length is over $2\frac{1}{8}$, which is the
halfway point between 2 and $2\frac{1}{4}$.

To the nearest $\frac{1}{8}$ in., the nail is $2\frac{1}{8}$ in. long.

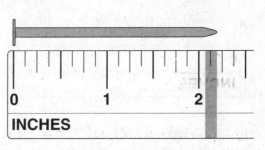

The measurement to the nearest $\frac{1}{8}$ in. is
the closest to the actual measurement.

Measure each segment to the nearest $\frac{1}{2}$, $\frac{1}{4}$, and $\frac{1}{8}$ in.

1. ├───────────────────┤

_____ , _____ , _____

2. ├─────────────────────────┤

_____ , _____ , _____

3. ├──────┤

_____ , _____ , _____

4. Number Sense A beetle is just over $1\frac{5}{8}$ in. long. How long
is the beetle to the nearest $\frac{1}{2}$ in.?

_____

Capacity and Customary Units

Capacity is the amount that a container can hold. Capacity is measured in teaspoons, tablespoons, fluid ounces, cups, pints, quarts, and gallons, from smallest to largest.

  1 tablespoon (tbsp) = 3 teaspoons (tsp)

  1 fluid ounce (fl oz) = 2 tbsp

  1 cup (c) = 8 fl oz

  1 pint (pt) = 2 c

  1 quart (qt) = 2 pt

  1 gallon (gal) = 4 qt

A container that holds 2 gal will hold more than 2 qt. A container that holds 20 c will hold less than 20 pt.

Choose the most appropriate unit or units to measure the capacity of each. Write tsp, tbsp, fl oz, c, pt, qt, or gal.

1. eye dropper _____   **2.** bathtub _____

3. milk carton _____   **4.** water tower _____

5. teacup _____   **6.** flour in a recipe _____

7. Reasoning Would a teaspoon be a good tool for measuring the amount of water in a bathtub? Explain why or why not.

_____

_____

Blood The adult human body contains about 5 qt of blood.

8. Are there more or less than 5 pt of blood in a human adult?

9. Are there more or less than 5 gal of blood in a human adult?

_____   _____

Name_____

Weight and Customary Units

There are 16 ounces (oz) in 1 pound (lb).

There are 2,000 lb in 1 ton (T).

You use ounces to weigh smaller things, like a tomato.

You use pounds to weigh things like a heavy box.

You use tons to weigh very large or heavy things, like a rocket.

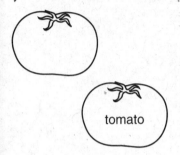

tomato

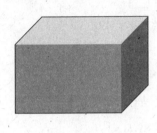

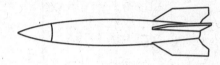

Choose the most appropriate unit to measure the weight of each. Write oz, lb, or T.

1. car _____

2. computer _____

3. bowling ball _____

4. onion _____

5. dinosaur _____

6. vacuum cleaner _____

7. Reasoning A hippo weighs about 5,000 lb. Does the same hippo weigh more or less than 5,000 oz?

_____

8. Would you most likely measure a leaf using ounces, pounds, or tons? Explain.

_____

_____

_____

_____

Changing Units and Comparing Measures

How to change customary units:

To change larger units to smaller units, multiply.	To change smaller units to larger units, divide.
12 yd = ☐ ft	20 qt = ☐ gal
Think: 1 yd = 3 ft	Think: 1 gal = 4 qt
12 × 3 = 36	20 ÷ 4 = 5
So, 12 yd = 36 ft.	So, 20 qt = 5 gal.

How to compare measures:

Compare 2 mi ◯ 11,000 ft.

Step 1 Change to the same units.	**Step 2** Compare.
2 mi ☐ 11,000 ft	10,560 ft < 11,000 ft
1 mi = 5,280 ft	So, 2 mi < 11,000 ft.
Think: 5,280 × 2 = 10,560	
2 mi = 10,560 ft	

Find each missing number.

1. 50 pt = _____ qt

2. 10 tbsp = _____ fl oz

3. 2 lb 1 oz = _____ oz

4. 9 yd = _____ ft

5. 3 gal = _____ qt

6. 12 tsp = _____ tbsp

Compare. Write > or < for each ◯.

7. 8 qt ◯ 3 gal

8. 10 lb ◯ 100 oz

9. 2 mi ◯ 5,000 yd

10. Reasoning The heart of a giraffe is 2 ft long and can weigh as much as 24 lb. How many ounces can the heart of a giraffe weigh?

_____

Name_____

Exact Answer or Estimate

The Fundraiser There are 296 students signed up to attend a fundraiser at the school gym. Each student will receive an 8 oz bag of popcorn and a drink. Sheri is making the popcorn, and has made 3,000 oz so far. Does she need to make more?

What are you trying to find?

Is 3,000 oz enough popcorn for 296 students to each receive 8 oz?

Do you need an exact answer or an estimate?

You don't need to know the exact amount of popcorn needed for 296 students. You just need to know if there is enough already, so an estimate is OK. Since $300 \times 8 = 2,400$; 3,000 oz is enough.

Tell whether an exact answer is needed or if an estimate is enough. Then solve.

1. A picture measures 11 in. $\times$ 14 in. Michael wants to make a frame for the picture out of wood. He has a 5 ft piece of wood he would like to use. Is the wood long enough to make a frame?

_____

_____

2. Theo is a schoolteacher. He needs to order buses for a third-grade field trip. Each bus can hold 70 students. There are a total of 97 third graders. If Theo ordered 2 buses for the trip, will all of the students be able to fit?

_____

_____

3. Jane bought 7 notebooks. If each notebook costs $2, how much did Jane spend?

_____

Name_____

Facts Galore!

A full-sized whale needs to eat more than 2 T of food every day. Is 3,750 lb of food a day enough for a full-sized whale?

Remember, to compare measures you must first change to the same units.

  1 T = 2,000 lb, so 2 T = 4,000 lb.

  3,750 lb < 4,000 lb

So, 3,750 lb is not enough food for the whale.

Solve.

The Eiffel Tower is 984 ft tall and weighs 7,300 T.

1. How many yards tall is the Eiffel Tower?   _____

2. How many pounds does the Eiffel Tower weigh?

_____

3. Presidents Cleveland, Coolidge, Eisenhower, Lincoln, and Nixon were from the states of California, Kentucky, New Jersey, Texas, and Vermont. Coolidge and Cleveland were not from California, Kentucky, or Texas. Lincoln was from Kentucky. Nixon was not from Texas. Cleveland's home state was New Jersey. Complete the chart to find out what state Eisenhower was from.

	CA	NJ	TX	VT	KY
Cleveland					
Coolidge					
Eisenhower					
Lincoln					
Nixon					

Decimals and Fractions

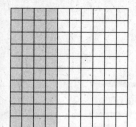

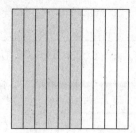

Fraction: $\frac{40}{100}$ Decimal: 0.40   Fraction: $\frac{6}{10}$ Decimal: 0.6

Writing fractions as decimals:

Write $\frac{4}{5}$ as a decimal.

$$\overset{\times\,20}{\overset{\frown}{\frac{4}{5}}} = \underset{\underset{\times\,20}{\smile}}{\frac{80}{100}}$$

80 parts out of 100 is 0.80.

So, $\frac{4}{5} = 0.80$.

Writing decimals as fractions:

Write 0.8 as a fraction in simplest form.

0.8 is eight tenths or $\frac{8}{10}$.

$$\overset{\div\,2}{\overset{\frown}{\frac{8}{10}}} = \underset{\underset{\div\,2}{\smile}}{\frac{4}{5}}$$

So, $0.8 = \frac{4}{5}$.

Write a fraction and a decimal for the part of each grid that is shaded.

1.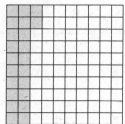

2.

_____   _____

Write each fraction as a decimal.

3. $\frac{6}{10}$ _____   **4.** $\frac{75}{100}$ _____   **5.** $1\frac{1}{10}$ _____

Write each decimal as a fraction or a mixed number in simplest form.

6. 0.3 _____   **7.** 0.95 _____   **8.** 7.7 _____

Decimal Place Value

There are different ways to represent the decimal 1.35.

Number line:

1.30 1.31 1.32 1.33 1.34 1.35 1.36 1.37 1.38 1.39

Place-value chart:

Ones		Tenths	Hundredths
1	.	3	5

Expanded form: $1 + 0.3 + 0.05$

Standard form: 1.35

Word form: one and thirty-five hundredths

Write each number in standard form.

1. Two and seventeen hundredths _____

2. $80 + 7 + 0.09$ _____

Write the word form and tell the value of the underlined digit for each number.

3. 4.<u>1</u>6 _____

_____

4. <u>2</u>.08 _____

_____

5. 9.9<u>4</u> _____

_____

The world's largest dog biscuit measured 2.35 m long, 577 cm wide, and 2.54 cm thick.

6. Write the thickness of the dog biscuit in expanded form.

_____

Comparing and Ordering Decimals

Compare 0.87 to 0.89.

First, begin at the left. Find the first place where the numbers are different.

0.87

0.89

The numbers are the same in the tenths places, so look to the next place.

The first place where the numbers are different is the hundredths place. Compare 7 hundredths to 9 hundredths.

0.07 < 0.09, so 0.87 < 0.89

Compare. Write >, <, or = for each ◯.

1. 0.36 ◯ 0.76

2. 5.1 ◯ 5.01

3. 1.2 ◯ 1.20

4. 6.55 ◯ 6.6

5. 0.62 ◯ 0.82

6. 4.71 ◯ 4.17

Order the numbers from least to greatest.

7. 1.36, 1.3, 1.63

8. 0.42, 3.74, 3.47

_____

_____

9. 6.46, 6.41, 4.6

10. 0.3, 0.13, 0.19, 0.31

_____

_____

11. Number Sense Which is greater, 8.0 or 0.8? Explain.

_____

_____

_____

_____

Rounding Decimals

Here is how to round decimals:

		Round 5.23 to the nearest whole number.	Round 3.67 to the nearest tenth.
Step 1	Find the rounding place.	5.23 ↑ 5 is in the ones place.	3.67 ↑ 6 is in the tenths place.
Step 2	Look at the digit to the right. If it is 5 or more, change to the next greatest digit. If it is less than 5, leave the number as it is.	5.23 ↑ Leave the number as it is because 2 < 5. 5.23 rounds to 5.	3.67 ↑ Change 6 to 7, because 7 > 5. 3.67 rounds to 3.7.

Round each number to the nearest whole number.

1. 27.93 _____   **2.** 0.8 _____   **3.** 7.49 _____   **4.** 63.1 _____

Round each number to the nearest tenth.

5. 63.25 _____   **6.** 0.47 _____

7. 11.14 _____   **8.** 1.92 _____

9. 33.08 _____   **10.** 27.64 _____

11. Number Sense Ashley was asked to round 79.37 to the nearest tenth. She answered 79.3. Is her answer correct? Explain.

_____

_____

_____

_____

Estimating Decimal Sums and Differences

To estimate, you change numbers to ones that are easier to add and subtract.

Estimate $11.7 + 3.8$.

Estimate by rounding to the nearest whole number.

11.7	+	3.8		
↓		↓		
12	+	4	=	16

So, $11.7 + 3.8$ is about 16.

Estimate $12.9 - 7.1$.

Estimate by rounding to the nearest whole number.

12.9	–	7.1		
↓		↓		
13	–	7	=	6

So, $12.9 - 7.1$ is about 6.

Estimate each sum or difference.

1. $7.12 + 8.64$ _____

2. $12.74 - 6.11$ _____

3. $22.91 + 4.86$ _____

4. $17.4 - 12.8$ _____

5. $19.8 + 7.12$ _____

6. $31.22 - 18.3$ _____

7.   9.3
      $+ 6.27$

8.   8.4
      $- 3.1$

9.   4.13
      $- 1.68$

10.   0.31
      $+ 0.74$

11.   24.7
      $+ \ \ 3.88$

12.   51.99
      $+ 11.11$

13.   24.24
      $- 12.81$

14.   0.79
      $+ 1.88$

15. Number Sense Explain why 20 is NOT a reasonable estimate for $33.71 - 17.25$.

_____

_____

Using Grids to Add and Subtract Decimals

Adding decimals using a hundredths grid:

Add 0.32 + 0.17.

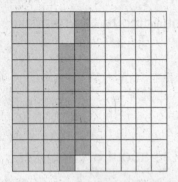

Step 1: Shade 32 squares to show 0.32.

Step 2: Use a different color. Shade 17 squares to show 0.17.

Step 3: Count all the squares that are shaded. How many hundredths are shaded in all? Write the decimal for the total shaded squares: 0.49.

So, 0.32 + 0.17 = 0.49.

Subtracting decimals using a hundredths grid:

Subtract 0.61 − 0.42.

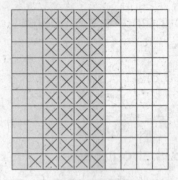

Step 1: Shade 61 squares to show 0.61.

Step 2: Cross out 42 squares to show 0.42.

Step 3: Count the squares that are shaded but not crossed out. Write the decimal: 0.19.

So, 0.61 − 0.42 = 0.19.

Add or subtract. You may use grids to help.

1. 0.22 + 0.35 = _____

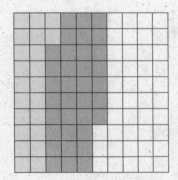

2. 0.52 − 0.41 = _____

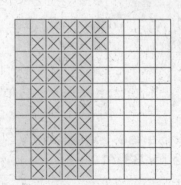

Name_____

Adding and Subtracting Decimals

Add 12.8 + 52.64.

First, estimate 13 + 53 = 66.

Step 1	Step 2	Step 3	Step 4
Line up the decimal points. Write zeros as place holders, if necessary.	Add the hundredths. Regroup if necessary.	Add the tenths. Regroup if necessary.	Add the ones, then the tens. Place the decimal point.

		1	1
12.80	12.80	12.80	12.80
+ 52.64	+ 52.64	+ 52.64	+ 52.64
	4	4 4	65.44

Remember,
12.8 = 12.80.

The sum 65.44 is reasonable because it is close to the estimate of 66.

Subtract 68.2 − 41.05.

First, estimate 70 − 40 = 30.

Step 1	Step 2	Step 3	Step 4
Line up the decimal points. Write zeros as place holders, if necessary.	Subtract hundredths. Regroup if necessary.	Subtract tenths. Regroup if necessary.	Continue subtracting ones and tens, regrouping as necessary. Place the decimal point.

	1 10	1 10	1 10
68.20	68.2̸0	68.2̸0	68.2̸0
− 41.05	− 41.05	− 41.05	− 41.05
	5	1 5	27.15

Remember,
68.2 = 68.20.

The sum 27.15 is reasonable because it is close to the estimate of 30.

1.   12.51
   +   6.43

2.   5.8
   + 0.65

3.   8.97
   − 5.61

4.   15.8
   − 12.15

5. **Estimation** Estimate the sum of 35.67 and 9.51.

PROBLEM-SOLVING STRATEGY

Solve a Simpler Problem

Squares A student is making a pattern of squares out of cotton balls. Each unit on a side of the pattern is made up of 2 cotton balls. How many cotton balls will the student need to make a pattern that is 4 units high and 4 units wide?

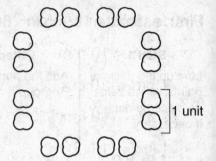

1 unit

Read and Understand

Step 1: What do you know?

There are 2 cotton balls in each unit. The square is 4 units high and 4 units wide.

Step 2: What are you trying to find?

How many cotton balls are needed in all

Plan and Solve

Step 3: What strategy will you use?

Strategy: Solve a simpler problem

Problem 1: How many cotton balls are needed for a 1-unit by 1-unit square?

8 cotton balls are needed for a 1-unit square.

Problem 2: How many cotton balls are needed for a 2-unit by 2-unit square?

16 cotton balls are needed for a 2-unit square.

There are 2 cotton balls for each unit on the side. There are always 4 sides, so the pattern is the number of units in each side, multiplied by 2 cotton balls, multiplied by 4 sides.

Answer: 32 cotton balls are needed.

Look Back and Check

Step 4: Is your work correct?

Yes, all of my computations are correct, and I saw the correct pattern.

---

1. Joan works for 6 hr each weekday, and 8 hr total on the weekends. She earns $6 an hour on weekdays and $9 an hour on weekends. How much money does she earn each week?

Name_____

Length and Metric Units

Metric units are used to estimate and measure length.

Metric Units of Length

    1 cm = 10 mm

    1 dm = 10 cm

    1 m = 100 cm

    1 km = 1,000 m

Find the length to the nearest centimeter.

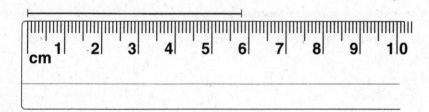

Measured to the nearest centimeter, the segment is 6 cm long.

Estimate first. Then find each length to the nearest centimeter.

1. _____

2. _____

Choose the most appropriate unit to measure each. Write mm, cm, dm, m, or km.

3. length of a finger _____

4. length of a football _____

5. width of a big toe _____

6. length of the lunchroom _____

7. distance between Paris and London _____

8. Number Sense The distance across a field is 20 m. Is the distance across the same field greater than or less than 20 km?

_____

_____

Capacity and Metric Units

Capacity is the amount of liquid that an object can hold. The metric system of measurement uses the units liter (L) and milliliter (mL).

You would use liters to measure the amount of water in a water bottle or the amount of gasoline in a gas can.

A milliliter is a very small unit of measurement. There are 5 mL of liquid in a teaspoon. You would use milliliters to measure small amounts of liquid, such as measuring how much medicine to give a baby.

1 L is the same as 1,000 mL.

Choose the most appropriate unit to use to measure the capacity of each.

1. thimble   _____

2. kitchen sink   _____

3. coffee cup   _____

4. bucket of water for a horse   _____

5. **Number Sense** A container holds 5 L of fluid. Does it hold more than or less than 5 mL of fluid?

_____

6. Mr. Burke has a 1 L container of oil. He poured 750 mL of oil into his lawn mower. How many mL are left in the container?

_____

7. A bottle is filled with saline solution for eyes. Is the bottle more likely to hold 15 mL of solution or 1 L of solution?

_____

_____

Mass and Metric Units

The metric units for mass are grams (g) and kilograms (kg).

    1 kg = 1,000 g

A cherry or a pen might have the mass of 1 g.

A kitten or watermelon might have the mass of 1 kg.

Choose the most appropriate unit to measure the mass of each.
Write g or kg.

1. lawn mower   _____   **2.** pumpkin   _____

3. child   _____   **4.** gold ring   _____

5. robin's egg   _____   **6.** cannonball   _____

7. cement block   _____   **8.** spool of thread _____

9. Number Sense Which is greater, 850 g or 1 kg?

_____

10. The mass of a certain window is 18.6 kg. What is the mass
of 2 of the same windows together?

_____

_____

11. The mass of a horse is 180.82 kg. The mass of the horse's
sister is 275.6 kg. How much larger is the mass of the
sister than that of the first horse?

_____

_____

_____

Changing Units and Comparing Measures

How to change metric units:

To change larger units to smaller units, multiply.

    6 kg = □ g

    Think: 1 kg = 1,000 g

    6 × 1,000 = 6,000

So, 6 kg = 6,000 g.

To change smaller units to larger units, divide.

    200 mm = □ cm

    Think: 1 cm = 10 mm

    200 ÷ 10 = 20

So, 200 mm = 20 cm.

How to compare measures:

Compare 2 m 73 cm to 285 cm.

Step 1: Change to the same units.

Think: 1 m = 100 cm

200 + 73 = 273 cm

2 m 73 cm = 273 cm

Step 2: Compare.

273 cm < 285 cm

So, 2 m 73 cm < 285 cm.

Find each missing number.

1. 32,000 g = _____ kg

2. 9 cm 3 mm = _____ mm

3. 1 m 45 cm = _____ cm

Compare. Write > or < for each.

4. 90 g ◯ 9 kg

5. 1,750 mL ◯ 2 L

6. 12 m 6 cm ◯ 126 cm

7. Number Sense How many meters are in 13 km? _____

PROBLEM-SOLVING SKILL
Writing to Explain

Airplanes The Paper Airplane Club at school was having a contest to see whose paper airplane could fly the farthest. Before the contest started, students were allowed two practice flights to test their planes. The results are shown at the right.

Student	Flight 1	Flight 2
Cheryl	3 m	2 m 10 cm
Kenya	6 m 3 cm	7 m
Mario	36 cm	1 m 5 cm

Use the data in the table to predict who will win the contest.

Writing a Math Explanation

- Make sure your prediction is stated clearly.

- Use steps to make your explanation clear.

- Show and explain carefully how you used the numbers to make your prediction.

Example

I think Kenya will win. Here is why.

1. I looked at the results of the two test flights. Her plane flew over 6 m both times.

2. Cheryl's and Mario's planes both flew much less each flight. Mario's plane barely flew more than 1 m.

3. When they fly their planes in the contest, Kenya's plane will likely fly around 6 m and the other planes will fly less than that, so Kenya's plane should win.

---

1. The softball league is going to have a playoff. All 4 teams are included. During the season, each team played 30 games. Team A won 17 games, Team B won 29, Team C won 16, and Team D won 7. Predict which team will win the championship. Tell why.

_____

_____

_____

Temperature

Thermometers are used to measure the temperature.
Often thermometers will have both the degrees
Celsius (°C) and the degrees Fahrenheit (°F) scales
on them.

Reading a thermometer:

The scale on the right side of the thermometer
is the Celsius scale. The temperature is
about 15°C.

The scale on the left side of the thermometer
is the Fahrenheit scale. The temperature is
about 58°F.

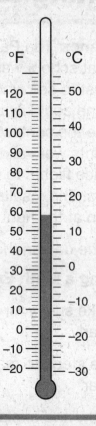

Read each thermometer. Write the temperature in °C and in °F.

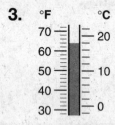

1.   2.   3.

_____

4. **Number Sense** Are you more likely to ice skate on a lake
   when the temperature outside is 30°C or 30°F? Explain.

_____

_____

_____

_____

Name_____

Shark!

About how long is a basking shark to the nearest whole meter?

First find the rounding place.

12.3

2 is in the ones place.

Then look at the digit to the right.

12.3

3 < 5, so leave the number as it is.

So, the basking shark is about 12 m long.

Sharks

Shark	Length (meters)
Whale shark	15 m
Basking shark	12.3 m
Great white shark	6.4 m
Piked dogfish shark	1.6 m
Spined pygmy shark	21 cm
Pygmy ribbontail cat shark	16 cm

Use the chart above to solve each problem.

1. How many centimeters longer is the great white shark than the spined pygmy shark?

   _____

2. How many millimeters longer is the spined pygmy shark than the pygmy ribbontail cat shark?

   _____

3. Write the length of the whale shark in centimeters and millimeters.

   _____

4. The piked dogfish shark is the most common shark. Is the piked dogfish shark more likely to weigh 200 kg or 200 g?

   _____

5. If 2 great white sharks were placed end to end, what would their total length be?

   _____

Inequalities on a Number Line

To solve an inequality, you must find the value that makes the inequality true.

For example: $x < 4$ is an inequality. This means "x is less than 4."

What numbers make the inequality true? What numbers are less than 4?

    0, 1, 2, and 3 are all less than 4. They can solve the inequality.

    5, 6, and 7 are greater than 4. They cannot solve the inequality.

To graph the solutions to the inequality $x < 4$, first draw an open circle at 4 on the number line. Then draw an arrow over the solutions.

Name three solutions to each inequality and graph all the solutions on a number line.

1. $b > 5$

_____

2. $a < 9$

_____

3. $d > 0$

_____

4. $m < 13$

_____

5. Number Sense Could $7 - 4$ be a solution to the inequality $c < 2$? Explain.

_____

Translating Words to Equations

When you are translating words to equations, the words give clues about which operation you should use in the equation.

The words *plus*, *added*, and *more* tell you that you should use addition.

Sentence	Equation
y plus 9 is equal to 17.	$y + 9 = 17$

The words *minus*, *less than*, and *difference* tell you that you should use subtraction.

Sentence	Equation
8 less than m is 7.	$m - 8 = 7$

Divided by and *equally between* refer to division, and *product*, *times*, and *each* refer to multiplication.

Sentence	Equation
16 split equally between n is 4.	$16 \div n = 4$
5 times n is 25.	$5n = 25$

Write an equation for each sentence.

1. 12 times t is 132.

_____

2. 8 minus r equals 2.

_____

3. 70 plus w is 102.

_____

4. 100 divided by x is 10.

_____

Write an equation for the problem.

5. Number Sense Harry had $45 and gave $5 to his brother. How much money does Harry have left?

_____

Equations and Graphs

Use the equation $y = x + 2$. Find the value of y if $x = 3$.

First substitute 3 for x. $y = 3 + 2$

Then add. $y = 5$

So when $x = 3$, $y = 5$.

x	y
0	2
1	3
2	4
3	5

Here is a table of values made from the equation $y = x + 2$.

The table of values can be used to make a graph of the line $y = x + 2$. Plot each ordered pair from the table. For example, (0, 2).

Then connect the plotted points with a straight line.

Other ordered pairs on the graph of the equation are (4, 6), (5, 7), and (6, 8).

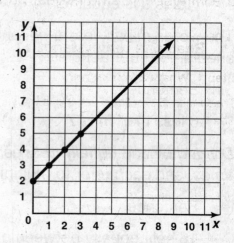

Use the equation $y = 3x + 1$ to find the value of y for each value of x.

1. $x = 0$ _____

2. $x = 2$ _____

3. $x = 4$ _____

4. $x = 6$ _____

5. Graph the equation $y = x - 2$ on the coordinate grid at the right.

6. List five ordered pairs on the graph of the equation $y = x + 9$.

_____

_____

_____

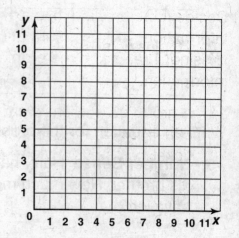

PROBLEM-SOLVING SKILL

Extra or Missing Information

Butterflies The largest butterfly is the female Queen Alexandra Birdwing butterfly, which has a wingspan of 32 cm. The next largest butterfly is the Goliath Birdwing, which has a wingspan of 28 cm. The smallest butterfly is the Western Pygmy Blue, which has a wingspan of only 1.5 cm. How many centimeters longer is the wingspan of the largest butterfly than that of the smallest?

Read and Understand

Step 1: What do you know?

The Queen Alexandra Birdwing is the largest and has a 32 cm wingspan.
The Western Pygmy Blue is the smallest and has a wingspan of 1.5 cm.

Step 2: What are you trying to find?

How much longer is the wingspan of the largest butterfly than that of the smallest butterfly?

Plan and Solve

Step 3: Find and use the needed information.

32 cm − 1.5 cm = 30.5 cm. The difference between the longest wingspan and the shortest wingspan is 30.5 cm.

The wingspan of the Goliath Birdwing was extra information.

Decide if the problem has extra information or not enough information. Tell any information that is not needed or that is missing. Then solve the problem if you have enough information.

1. A group of 12 teens went skiing. Three of them took a chairlift up the hill, and the rest used the T-bar. The chairlift ticket costs $3.00 more than the T-bar ticket. How many teens used the T-bar?

   _____

   _____

Understanding Probability

Probability is the chance that a certain event will happen.
Events can be likely, unlikely, impossible, or certain.

Spinner A

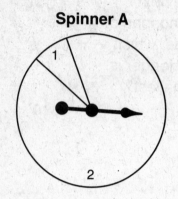

Spinner B

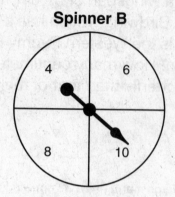

In Spinner A, it is likely that the number 2 will be spun. Over half
of the spinner area is number 2.

In Spinner A, spinning a 1 is unlikely.

In Spinner A, spinning a 3 is impossible. There is no 3 on the spinner.

In Spinner B, spinning an even number is certain. All of the
numbers are even.

Tell whether each event is likely,
unlikely, impossible, or certain.

Spinner C

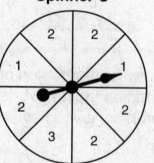

Spinner D

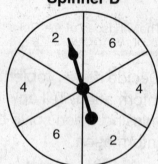

1. Spinning a 2 on Spinner C

   _____

2. Spinning a 2 on Spinner D

   _____

3. Spinning an even number on Spinner D   _____

4. Spinning a 4 on Spinner C   _____

5. **Reasoning** Describe an event using Spinner D that would
   be impossible.

   _____

Listing Outcomes

List all the possible outcomes for the spinners shown.

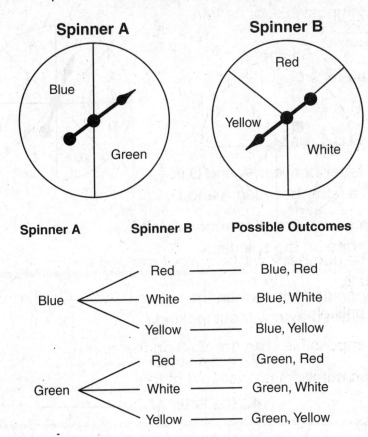

List all the possible outcomes for selecting a marble from each box, without looking.

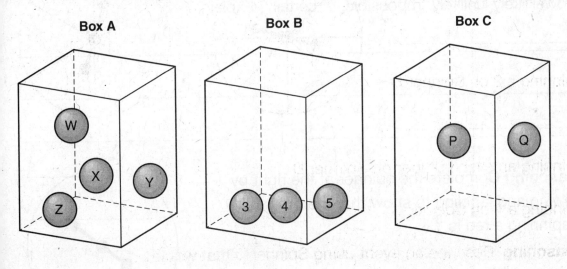

1. Box A _____

2. Boxes B and C _____

Name_____

Finding Probability

You can write a fraction to describe the probability of an event.

Probability = $\dfrac{\text{number of favorable outcomes}}{\text{number of possible outcomes}}$

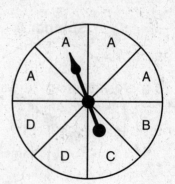

The probability of spinning an A is $\frac{4}{8}$ or $\frac{1}{2}$.

The probability of spinning a B is $\frac{1}{8}$.

The probability of spinning a D is $\frac{2}{8}$, or $\frac{1}{4}$.

The probability of spinning a letter between A and D is $\frac{8}{8}$, or 1. It is certain you will spin a letter between A and D.

The probability of spinning an L is $\frac{0}{8}$, or 0. It is impossible to spin an L, because there isn't one on the spinner.

Write the probability of drawing each letter when the letters from the word MATHEMATICS are drawn without looking.

1. a vowel _____

2. not a vowel _____

3. a capital letter _____

4. the letter *M* _____

5. the letter *L* _____

6. the letter *C* _____

7. **Number Sense** In the problem above, is the event of drawing a vowel likely, unlikely, impossible, or certain? Explain.

_____

_____

_____

8. **Reasoning** Complete the spinner at the right by drawing and labeling to show that the probability of spinning a red is $\frac{3}{4}$.

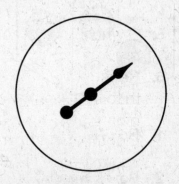

Name_____

Making Predictions

Predict the number of times the letter *p* will
be drawn when you pick a letter 15 times.
The letter is returned to the bag after
each pick.

To make the prediction, take the probability,
$\frac{1}{3}$, and find an equivalent fraction with the
number of picks in the denominator.

$$\frac{1}{3} = \frac{}{15}$$

To go from a 3 to a 15, you multiply by 5.
To make an equivalent fraction, you must
multiply the numerator and denominator
by the same number. $1 \times 5 = 5$

$$\frac{1}{3} = \frac{5}{15}$$

The prediction is that out of 15 draws, a *p* will be drawn 5 times.

Use the spinner to predict how many times each
letter will be spun.

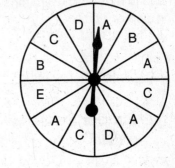

1. *D* when you spin 12 times

   _____

2. *E* when you spin 48 times

   _____

3. *A* when you spin 9 times _____

4. *B* when you spin 60 times _____

5. *C* when you spin 100 times _____

6. **Reasoning** A meteorologist predicted
   that it would rain 1 out of 3 days this
   month. If there are 30 days in the
   month, about how many days would
   you expect it to rain? _____

Name_____

Work Backward

Morning Routine Brenda takes 30 min to get dressed for school. She eats breakfast for 20 min more, then walks to school. It takes Brenda 15 min to walk to school. Brenda needs to be at school by 8:55 A.M. What time is the latest she should get out of bed in the morning?

Read and Understand

Step 1: What do you know?

Brenda takes 30 min to get ready, 20 min for breakfast, and 15 min to walk to school. She must be at school by 8:55 A.M.

Step 2: What are you trying to find?

What time is the latest Brenda should get up?

Plan and Solve

Step 3: What strategy will you use?   **Strategy:** Work backward

Work backward from the end, doing the opposite of each step.

I need to move backward, or subtract from the school arrival time, one step at a time.

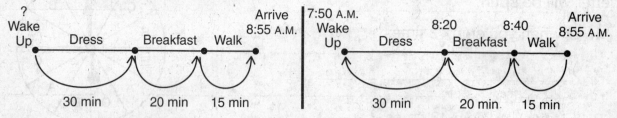

Brenda must get up by 7:50 A.M. at the latest to make it to school in time.

Look Back and Check

Step 4: Is your work correct?

Yes. If I follow the times forward, I end at 8:55 A.M.

---

1. When Christopher Columbus was 41 years old he sailed across the Atlantic Ocean for the first time. He went on his final expedition 10 years later, which took 2 years. He died 2 years after his final expedition ended, in 1506. What year was Columbus born?

Name_____

Veronica's Monday

Veronica rides the train every day to work. She needs to arrive at work by 9:00 A.M. It takes her 1 hr and 20 min to get ready for work. Her train ride lasts 30 min. What time is the latest that Veronica can get out of bed and still make it to work on time?

First, identify the time Veronica must arrive: 9:00 A.M.

Then work backwards using the information you know. Her train ride takes 30 min, and it takes her 1 hr 20 min to get ready. That is a total of 1 hr 50 min. One hour before 9:00 A.M. is 8:00 A.M., and 50 min before 8:00 A.M. is 7:10 A.M. So Veronica must get up by 7:10 A.M.

1. Veronica bought lunch, 2 sets of earrings, and a pair of tennis shoes at the mall. The earrings were $4.29 for each set and her tennis shoes were on sale for $22.79. She had $6.21 left when she was finished shopping. How much did she begin with?

   _____

   _____

   _____

   _____

2. In the afternoon, Veronica's coworker Keisha asked to borrow one of Veronica's pens. Veronica had 12 pens in her desk drawer. Three of them were black, 7 were blue, and 2 were red. What is the probability that Veronica will pick a red pen from her drawer?

   _____

3. Veronica worked 8 hr. Her manager asked her to work 3 more hours Tuesday than she did on Monday. Write an equation for *3 more than 8 hr.*

   _____